The Barbarian West

A.D. 400–1000

THE EARLY MIDDLE AGES

The Barbarian West

A.D. 400–1000

THE EARLY MIDDLE AGES

J. M. WALLACE-HADRILL

HARPER TORCHBOOKS ❦ *The Academy Library*
Harper & Row, Publishers • New York

THE BARBARIAN WEST

Printed in the United States of America

This volume was first published in the History series of the Hutchinson University Library, edited by Sir Maurice Powicke, in 1952, with a second, revised impression in 1962. It is here reprinted by arrangement with Hutchinson & Co., Ltd., London.

First HARPER TORCHBOOK edition published 1962

CONTENTS

MAPS

EUROPE

AT THE ACCESSION
OF JUSTINIAN

0   200 MILES

EN

Vistula

Elbe   Oder

SLAVS

GIANS

Ratisbon

Danube   LOMBARDS

AVARIANS

GEPIDS

OTHS

Sirmium   Danube

ROMAN

OSTROGOTHS

Rome

Constantinople

EMPIRE

"GEOGRAPHIA" LTD.

PREFACE

THE reader who requires a balanced introduction to the early Middle Ages will do best to turn without delay to the general books cited at the end of this volume, which, so far from seeking in any particular to replace, I gratefully build upon. In them, and in other books and articles that scholars will at once detect my debt to, will be found proper consideration of much that I have lacked space to cover, such, for example, as the history of barbarian Spain; or have relegated to a secondary position, like the development of the papacy, and early medieval administration; or I feel is still problematical, like the continuing pressure of Byzantium upon Western thought and action. These are integral parts of the full picture. Mine is only a sketch of certain aspects that interest me particularly, and which I think are sufficiently indicated by my title: the Roman West became barbarized; and yet it looked back. It remembered Rome. I ask myself not 'Why?' for that is obvious, but 'How?'

Some readers may find the chronology difficult to follow and, especially in the last chapter, may become confused by the names and numbers of many kings. To have added genealogical tables would materially have increased the length of the book; but instant help may be had from the books I cite in my bibliography or in such a work as Steinberg's *Historical Tables*, which is easily obtainable.

Sir Maurice Powicke, my mother and my wife have all, in different ways, given me help I could not have foregone; and I thank them for their generosity. I have also to thank the Cambridge University Press for permission to use Map 28a from the map volume of the Cambridge Medieval History.

A second impression (1957) has given me the opportunity to correct a few mistakes and to make certain slight additions to the text. I have added a further section to the bibliography which I have revised again for the fourth impression (1961).

J. M. W-H.

CHAPTER I

INTRODUCTORY

DURING the year A.D. 376 the Romans learned that the tribes living in the northern world, beyond the Danube frontier, were in motion. This kind of thing had happened before, and no doubt official quarters were reluctant to credit alarmist reports. But soon it became clear that the reports were anything but alarmist. The Huns, the most terrible of the barbarian peoples, had been stirred to life and were sweeping south towards the imperial frontiers, refugees streaming before them.

Our first task must be to distinguish some of the features of the civilization that was thus threatened.

We must observe, in the first place, that the time immediately preceding the irruption had been far from restful. The fourth century had, for the Romans, been an age of unquiet. That Peace of which the founder-Emperor, Augustus, had dreamt had slipped gradually away. The imperial frontiers had long since been advanced to a point where defence against external dangers was itself a burden sufficiently huge to create a new series of internal problems, economic and social. These did not, in themselves, prove fatal to the structure of the Empire; but they modified it. What were they?

In the first place, there was a labour problem. The defence in depth of an immense frontier had combined with the need to exploit all food-producing land to make every able-bodied man the object of strict and anxious state-supervision. But this, as so often happens, proved a self-destructive process; for the more rigidly men were pinned down to their war-time tasks the less able society proved to adapt itself to a rapidly changing situation. The Romans had inherited from the Greeks a strong sense of the rightness of social hierarchy. Each level of society had its function to perform; and between the levels the barriers were high. By and large, Rome had been built upon slave-labour and the material achievements of her prosperity upon the exploitation of unwilling hands that shared in few of the advantages. It thus followed that in the hour of need the slave population would bear no more of the added burden than it could possibly avoid. The Later Empire was a hotbed of servile unrest.

To us, other solutions to this great social problem easily suggest themselves. Why, for example, should not stricter economy have been practised on non-essential expenditure? Why should not more interest have been taken in labour-saving methods and devices? If they could reply, the Romans would probably answer that age-long reliance on plentiful slave-labour is not conducive to technical inventiveness.

As for cutting down on expenditure, no Emperor could have considered it for a moment. Fine towns and great households were the very substance of the Roman way of living. And so the Emperors continued to live beyond their means because the alternative was not to live at all. Nor, in any case, can we be certain that retrenchment at home would have done much to help Rome meet the vast additional costs of military defence on a tremendous frontier.

But rigidity of outlook and lack of adaptability showed themselves in most fields of social activity. Growing fiscal demands on the soil were met with declining, though by no means steadily declining, productivity. Endemic plague and the casualties of war further reduced an agricultural population to which the alternative of mass-brigandage was already making its appeal. Documents of the fourth century show us agricultural land going out of cultivation in every part of the Roman world, and particularly in the frontier areas. The great independent landlords saw what was happening and did what they could to check the process. Sometimes they were successful. The imperial administration also saw, but could devise no general alternative to the policy of settling the deserted properties and filling the legions with clans of barbarians.

Here, then, were some of the material difficulties that modified the shape and nature of the Empire in the fourth century; though of course there were others—most of them with roots deep in the past.

What did the Romans make of it? They were very used to

speculation, not about themselves as persons so much as about society and the art of government. The shape of politics had always intrigued them, and the new threat to their Empire intensified the desire to speculate. They saw that their world was no longer the closed, Greek-speaking Mediterranean world of their ancestors, dominated by the traditions of the City of Rome. It was something bigger. Barbarians, tribesmen who knew no Greek and Latin, were part and parcel of it. Indeed, the great provinces themselves—Italy, Spain, Gaul— were already beginning to drift apart into distinct linguistic groups. Men were thinking and feeling as Europeans; but they still called themselves by the old name—Romans. Some of them were even occasionally making use of a new word, *Romania*, to describe the world they lived in. Self-consciousness of this sort was neither new nor un-natural, though it some- times strikes historians as such. But it is difficult to interpret. The writers whose works we depend on were writing in the hot atmosphere of crisis about the things they loved and hated. We must not expect, and do not find, dispassion. Instead, we find distortion—not least from the pens of the really great men, of whom the fourth century was by no means devoid. There are thus, at first glance, two Romes: the ramshackle, material Rome whose disintegration fascinates the economic historian; and the Rome of men's imagination that stands out bright with vitality from the written record. The task of the historian is to keep both Romes before him and to see that they are one.

As the material threat increased, so the Romans reflected with growing concern upon their cultural heritage. It was a complex heritage, having many facets. There was a religious facet—the cult of the pagan gods under whom the ancient world had grown up; a literary facet—the corpus of classical literature, prose and verse, of which a few strands have floated down to modern times; a legal facet, finally: and of this last something more must be said, difficult though it is.

The science of law was the bedrock of the Roman art of government. Both under the Republic and the Empire it had been zealously guarded and wisely adapted, somewhat after the fashion of our case-law. Its interpreters had not been narrow legal specialists but a learned aristocracy with the true end of law always before its eyes. So, to the ablest men of the fourth century, law and the science of law seemed their one incomparable legacy. In Gibbon's phrase, it was "the public reason of the Romans". The business of preserving such a heritage, the mere technical process of the conservation of tradition in manuscript form, inevitably involved a risk of petrification. Jurisprudence, like society itself, was running through a narrow channel and its shape was conditioned by the contours of the gorge. All the same, classical jurisprudence in this, its final phase was something more than a matter of haphazard salvage. It was a living art, as it had always been. The same century that produced the forebear[1] of the great law books of the Emperors Theodosius II and Justinian produced also a new venture, the collation of Mosaic with Roman Law. Furthermore, the teaching of the law schools was going on all over Europe, perhaps without as much interruption as was once supposed, and the Western legal tradition was, like the Eastern, still in the keeping of learned men, trained to love jurisprudence as the fine flower of Antiquity.

Social unrest had not proved very propitious to the established pagan cults of the Empire. The gods—and they were many—who had blessed the Romans in victory were now being called to account, as gods often are when times are bad. Other religious cults were finding adherents; and one in particular, Christianity, was moving from strength to strength. It was no new-comer, of course. Modern research tends to show that Christian communities were established in the West at an earlier date than was once supposed possible. But by the close of the fourth century, the strictest exponents of the pagan Roman tradition looked upon Christianity as their most formidable enemy and the principal element in the social disintegration they strove to prevent.[2] The historian cannot accept their verdict as it stands, any more than he can accept without qualification the Christian retort that, so far from destroying

[1] It survives in what are known as the Vatican Fragments.
[2] It is not established that late classical paganism was moving inevitably towards Christianity, e.g. in its idea of the life after death, as instanced in the reliefs on sarcophagi, nor that the union of Christianity and classical culture in such great men as Lactantius and Prudentius pointed to a general and inevitable union.

Antiquity, Christianity preserved what was best in it. He will see that there is some truth in both assertions and will understand that both were the outcome of the deepest personal conviction.

If we are to appreciate the predominant rôle of Christianity in the threatened Empire and to see why the future of Europe was to be bound up with its victory, we shall need to glance at its early relationship with Rome. But first we must distinguish between three of the main strands in the Christian tradition. With one of them—Arianism—the Christianity practised by most of the Germanic invaders of the Western Empire, we shall be a good deal concerned later on, and can afford to neglect now. The others were the Western tradition (especially as propounded in Roman Africa) and the Eastern tradition.

Eastern Christianity had grown up at the cross-roads of Hellenistic and Oriental culture. It had absorbed something from both—sufficient indeed, to cause some to hold that the historic facts of the faith, uncomfortable facts, had been lost sight of. East Roman Christians saw the Kingdom of God on earth as a symbol of the Kingdom of Heaven and only secondly as an historic reality valid because of the facts of the Incarnation and the Resurrection. The greatest of the Eastern Fathers, Origen of Caesarea, had laid himself open to attack on these grounds. One critic, Porphyry, even argued that though he was a Christian in his manner of life, he was a Hellene in his religious thought and adapted Neoplatonism to the interpretation of the Scriptures. This, of course, was a gross oversimplification; Origen was one of a select company whose works taught Christians not to be afraid of pagan culture; but it had a germ of truth in it. Another Caesarean, Eusebius, took Origen's Christianity one stage further on its journey as a political and social force in writings that exercised a profound influence upon the Emperors. The Roman Emperor, for Eusebius, was the Expected One, the David of Christian prophecy, and his Empire the Messianic Kingdom.

Interpretations such as these go a long way to explain not the grip of Christianity upon the masses but the change in outlook of the Emperors themselves, from fierce hostility through spasmodic tolerance to personal, and finally official, acquiescence. War-leadership always brings with it an increase in power for public men, and a seeking after whatever will enhance personal prestige. The sacrosanct character of late Roman imperialism was of this kind. Origen and Eusebius made it possible for the Emperor Constantine to hail in Christianity, after proper trial, the most successful of the mystery cults, in which the magic of Christ's name wrought great things for his servants and ensured them prosperous peace and victorious war. In short, the official Christianity of Constantine and of the new capital he established at the eastern extremity of his Empire was Christianity with the detonator removed. Augustus was one kind of Pontifex Maximus, Constantine another.

In the West, Christianity took a different course and met a sterner enemy; for the City of Rome was the historic home of classical paganism. That contemporaries fully appreciated this contrast is indicated by the issue of certain memorial coins on the occasion of the dedication of the new Eastern capital, Constantinople. On them appear busts of the personifications of New and Old Rome. New Rome, a female figure, bears on her shoulder the globe, balanced upon the Cross of Christ. Old Rome is depicted as the She-Wolf with her twins, above whom hover the Pantheon of pagan Rome. Some of the coins even show shepherds approaching the cave of the twins, as if in active counterpart to the shepherds of Bethlehem.

Constantine had striven to make Old Rome the seat of the new imperial cult of Christ, and had lost. The West was full of Christians, but not Rome. The senatorial families had stood their ground and driven him to found his New Rome, where he could be as Christian as he pleased. Politically, this had the effect of completing the isolation of Constantine and his successors from Rome—a tendency already well developed through long years of campaigning. Cologne, Sirmium, Milan and Antioch had often proved more convenient centres than Rome; and to this list Constantinople, the ancient Byzantium, was now added. But in the sphere of religion the senatorial victory was still more momentous; for it tended to accentuate the isolation of Western Europe not only from the Emperors but also to some extent from the imperial brand of Christianity.

It left the way open to a sterner though by no means new influence, the Christianity of Africa. Of this influence Rome, not long since a Greek as much as a Latin city, was to be the chief purveyor to Latin Christendom. Greek was no longer the common language of the Mediterranean world; nor was Latin, except to educated men.

At this point we encounter the most formidable figure of Late Antiquity, St. Augustine, Bishop of Hippo and leader of the African Church in the early fifth century. He was the child and exponent of the African or Western Christian tradition. Intensely Roman though Africa was, it was a world that bred no compromise. African Christians had learned early to know their enemies, to damn the heretic and the pagan and to thrive on martyrdom, the proper food of fanaticism. They neither gave nor expected quarter. What is more important for our present purposes, they saw what Constantinople had sometimes missed—the historical significance of the Incarnation and the Resurrection. The New Testament, historically interpreted, offered believers peace after death but none before. "My Kingdom is not of this world."

Neither St. Augustine nor any of his African predecessors had the least doubt about the matter: Christianity was no state-religion and Emperor-worship (even if the Emperor were Christian) no substitute for direct communion between God and man through Christ. The coming of the Kingdom would be a consequence of the passing of the present order. Now, St. Augustine had a deep and subtle mind, and it would have been surprising had he not reflected much, at one time or another, upon theories of government, the functions of the state and the individual's rôle in the community. He was, after all, a son of Rome. And accordingly we find, scattered throughout his voluminous writings, discussion of such matters. It is possible, indeed, to isolate and collate these passages and to claim their author as the first political theorist of modern times. It is possible to see in him the conscious founder of the medieval church-state.

But St. Augustine could not foresee and was not interested in the Middle Ages. The task to which he gave his life was far more urgent. It was nothing less than the active defence of the full Christian doctrine; Christianity, not Christendom, was in danger. And this defence he undertook with all the art of ancient rhetoric.

What, it may be asked, could endanger Christianity now that it enjoyed imperial support? Its enemies were heresy and paganism. The former, endemic to Africa, was reinforced during St. Augustine's lifetime by the Vandal invaders; for they were Arians. The latter, reawakened emotionally in Rome, was finding new adherents and even converts from Christianity, particularly among the great families.

Something of the atmosphere may perhaps be recaptured from a celebrated passage of arms that took place in Rome in the year 382. The statue of Victory, symbol of Rome's glory since the time of Augustus, was removed from the altar in the senate house on imperial orders, to placate the Christians among the senators. This drew a measured protest from the spokesman of the pagan majority, Quintus Aurelius Symmachus. He said what he had to say without heat, as might have been expected of one who was an aristocrat, a scholar[1] and a public servant of high distinction. He asked, not for the suppression of Christianity but for toleration, by Christians, of the age-old cult of his class. It took all sorts to make a world, he seemed to think, and the Emperor surely stood to gain nothing by outlawing the rites practised and loved by his predecessors. Where would such iconoclasm end? Was not Roman religion (and here is the heart of the matter) inextricably tied to Roman law? If one part of the heritage went, must not others follow?

The day was saved for the Christians by the intervention of St. Ambrose, Bishop of Milan. Next to his younger contemporary, St. Augustine, St. Ambrose was the most distinguished Christian apologist of his generation. Trained in the imperial service, he had been chosen bishop of the great city of Milan by popular acclamation. Like many, perhaps most, other bishops of the time, he was the choice of the crowd. And now he came forward to deal with Symmachus. His letter

---

[1]The Symmachi were directly involved in the preserving of the text of Livy, all the oldest manuscripts of which are written in the same kind of uncial script and belong to the late fourth or early fifth century.

to the Emperor faced squarely the issues raised by the pagan, yet did so from an entirely different set of premises. The two men used the same words but attached to them different values. The religion of St. Ambrose was the single-hearted adoration of a God to whom the arts of civility were nothing, and who came on earth to bring his own peace, which was a sword. Christianity seen thus was not a game for intellectuals.

By contrast, the religion defended by Symmachus was no more (and no less) than the ritual aspect of the whole performance of civilized man. Perhaps that was why it required no martyrs. Paganism and Christianity were joined in battle, willingly or otherwise, along the whole line. The heritage of Antiquity was at stake.

But St. Ambrose's letter contained something else: a plain threat that the bishops would look upon the Emperor's decision as a kind of vote of confidence. If he pandered to the pagans— "they who were so little sparing of our blood and who made rubble of our churches"—he must not expect further support from Christian bishops. The priests of the new official imperial religion would withdraw from his service.

So the Christians had their way.

The Emperor did not, however, snuff out pagan Rome. Symmachus and his friends continued until 395 to serve the shrines of their gods, personally and at heavy cost. In another great city, Athens, instruction in the learned traditions of classical civilization remained in the hands of practising pagans. Christianity was safe, officially; but paganism, in its infinite variety, was not yet dead. That it might never die, but rather flare up into a new life, was the constant fear of Christian teachers like St. Ambrose and St. Augustine. It is not unlikely that the fall of Rome to the Goths in 410 was attributed by many to Rome's abandonment of her ancient cults. Men were again thinking of the example left them by the great apostate Emperor Julian, who had not so long ago turned back from Christ to the gods of his fathers. Indeed, there is evidence that Julian was something of a hero at the time of which we write. St. Augustine went out of his way to argue that the material prosperity of the Empire had no more been destroyed by Christianity than it had been created by paganism. Its collapse compelled him to define and state the Christian view of politics and history. When we turn, as we now must, to consider the material situation of the Western church at the close of the fourth century, let us keep in mind the Bishop of Hippo's waverers, with their cry "if only we sacrificed to the gods still!"

When St. Augustine wrote about the church on earth, as he often did, he was thinking of a human society and not of a territorial organization remotely resembling the medieval church. He was not even thinking of a church like that ruled by Pope Gregory the Great, a mere two centuries later. To begin with, the Bishops of Rome in the fourth century exercised no regular authority over other bishops; and again, church councils were spasmodic. The Church, in brief, had as yet no continuing means of common action. Each bishop ruled his community much as did the secular administrator of a *civitas*, or city district; and often the diocese and the *civitas* exactly corresponded. Further, just as several city districts were comprised in one province, so were several dioceses in one ecclesiastical province, and the heads of both kinds of province tended to reside in the same centre, or *metropolis*. In this way, the early Western church assumed the administrative shape of the Empire itself; and for this reason the bishops were often called upon to carry out the duties of their absentee secular colleagues. Bishops were city-dwellers, not countrymen. The crowds for whom their revolutionary message of personal salvation—salvation from an all-too-real world of demons—was intended, were the artisan and bourgeois populations of the industrial and commercial centres. There, in great towns like Milan and Carthage, alive with the social unrest that sharp contrasts of wealth and poverty necessarily breed, men of the stamp of St. Ambrose found an answer to their call. Nor is it difficult to see how the city-diocese proved a natural and convenient unit that needed no superior control; for its members were few enough to feel and act as a community, proud of its local traditions (of martyrs especially) and ready to follow its bishop where he led.

The same pattern of local autonomy is reflected in contemporary monastic communities. These, again, were a natural solution of the difficulty experienced by many Christians, men and women, in trying to lead Christian lives in an unsettled world. Imperial recognition of Christianity was not enough. Only by stepping aside from the complexities of secular life into communities of their own ordering could they find the peace they sought. A contemporary of St. Augustine, John Cassian, came from the eremetical solitudes of Egypt and the Holy Land to found at Marseilles a monastic community in which the fierce asceticism of his own masters was tempered by consideration for just such needs. His teaching marked out the future path of Western monasticism and his writings were to be the inspiration of a greater monk than himself, St. Benedict. But perhaps there was truth in the unkind comment of one observant pagan, Rutilius, that the monks were afraid of the favours as much as of the rigours of fortune. He really meant that the Christian and the Roman ways of life did not and could not mix. Christianity was not just a new name for Antiquity.

St. Augustine died inside the walls of his city-diocese while the Vandals encircled them. Not long afterwards, Hippo was to fall. Though his voice had rung through Christendom with a power not given to many, his most pressing task had been always the leadership of his own community, the Church of Hippo. When he thought of anything less than the whole community of Christian souls in the world, he thought of innumerable small communities, like his own, each with its own traditions and its own dangers. No wonder he feared for the future and put no trust in princes. To the end, he held fast to the doctrine that earthly kingdoms were, by their nature, doomed to self-destruction, for their objects were temporal. The earthly and the heavenly cities were for ever distinct, even if men in the nature of things found themselves members of both. Man's true end, and the only pursuit in which he could find happiness, was the service of the God revealed once, historically, in Christ. That service was love. There was no other love, no other service, no other happiness. The classical view of man's rôle in history had not much in common with this.

As he considers the Empire on the eve of the final barbarian thrust, the historian must be struck by nothing so forcibly as by the simple fact that a great many people were talking loudly about themselves and the things they believed in. Thunder was in the air, and they were frightened—not so much by the shortcomings of imperial administration, the changing shape of society and the barbarian threat (the things that strike the modern observer first), as by the sight of themselves, caught in the beam of a new, Christian, philosophy of history. Antiquity had explained itself to itself in terms of the interplay of two forces, human character and divine intervention, interpreted as fate or fortune. Together, these two had conspired to produce Eternal Rome, than which no greater state of material felicity was to be conceived. The mould was fixed. It was for mankind to fill it, from generation to generation. The trouble was to square this view with what actually happened in the world of events. How was it possible to square it with the history of the Later Empire—or, put succinctly, with the fact of Change? Christianity broke the mould by positing, in place of Eternal Rome, the eternal soul of each individual man and woman, the salvation of which was the proper business of life and compared with which the fate of empires was merely irrelevant.

In the clash of these half-seen, conflicting beliefs we have to pick our way in search of what we like to take as evidence. About us are men arguing for their lives—Christians against pagans, pagans against Christians. One special misfortune is that most of the anti-Christian polemic has perished. It did not interest the medieval scribe, and so is gone.

Parchment, papyrus, inscription, coin-legend and other kinds of evidence draw together to tell one story; but it is a terribly halting affair.

We can never be certain what was happening. But we can often guess what contemporaries thought was happening. We can see that the material troubles of their day had sharpened, without creating, their sense of un-ease both with the classical and with the Christian explanations of man's function in society. Some contended that Antiquity was passing away; others that it was not; some that Christianity and classical culture were good bed-fellows; others, including some Christians, that they were not. The history of the times is the fact rather than the outcome of this deep dispute.

And upon such a world the Huns fell.

CHAPTER II

MARE NOSTRUM

In the course of the third century A.D., two barbarian confederations became established in South-Eastern Europe. Literary sources tell us next to nothing about them, and archaeology not much more. At least we know that both comprised tribes of Eastern Germanic peoples—peoples with a long history of migration behind them.[1] They were old peoples, of set habits and complex traditions; barbarians, but not savages.

Both belonged to that section of the Germanic peoples called Goths. The eastern group, the Ostrogoths, occupied or controlled the steppe-lands lying between the Crimea and the rivers Don and Dniester. The Western group, or Visigoths, lived in the lands between the rivers Dniester and Danube. Both were largely pastoral peoples; and, like most such, must usually have found it a struggle to keep body and soul together. They could not, in fact, have done even this had they not traded regularly with the Roman Empire.

Away behind them, to the North, lived the Asiatic (non-Germanic) Huns; and it was the sudden, and still unexplained, irruption of these tribes that broke up the more stable Germanic confederations and set in motion a mass-movement of barbarian tribes which the imperial forces in the East found it impossible to hold. To absorb isolated tribes as settlers or as mercenaries was one thing: the Empire had had long experience of that; but suddenly to provide for thousands, quite another. An armed clash was unavoidable. It came on the 9th August, 378 near Adrianople, not far from the capital of the Eastern Empire. The imperial mercenaries were routed by a great cavalry charge

[1]The West Germans (those who in Tacitus' day occupied the Oder-Elbe region) were Franks, Alamans, Saxons, Frisians and Thuringians. The East Germans (distinct in dialect and customs from the West, and living east of the Oder) were Goths, Vandals, Burgundians, Gepids and Lombards. A third, or Northern, group—the Scandinavians—had never left home.

and the Emperor himself killed. It was a disaster of the first magnitude.

Thereafter, the Eastern provinces were open to devastation and plunder, in which Goths and Huns and subordinate tribes, driven on by famine, all played their part. It was as much as Constantinople could do to preserve itself from destruction.

The West, also, was open to attack. With the details of that attack we cannot concern ourselves. It must be sufficient to say that the Western Empire was fully aware of the danger in which it stood and took what measures it could to deflect the force of the breaking wave and to canalize its waters. It was not wholly unsuccessful. But the cost was no less than the complete barbarization of the army, and the surrender, by the Emperors, of all effective power into the hands of barbarian chieftains. In the consequent confusion—it was not quite as chaotic as is sometimes thought—the line of public policy is often hard to distinguish; but behind the struggle for self-preservation, it is there. Certain provinces, coasts and towns were always considered worth fighting for, while others were not. The Western Emperors, secure behind the marshes of Ravenna, were puppets perhaps. But their strings were worth pulling.

The greatest of the barbarian chieftains to defend the West against his own kind was the Vandal, Stilicho. Rising rapidly in the military hierarchy, he secured his position by marrying the niece of the Emperor Theodosius I who, dying, left the Empire divided between his two sons. Stilicho he designated guardian to the younger (Honorius), to whom fell the West. But a decade of skilful manœuvre against the Goths could not endear Stilicho to the Romans. He saved Rome twice (it fell to Alaric soon after his death), yet he remained the scapegoat of Roman writers, who preferred to see in him the man who sold the pass. Why was this? Partly, it seems, because he was ready to compromise with the Goths in an attempt to wrest the much-coveted eastern parts of Illyricum from the control of Constantinople. Partly, too, because his concentration on Italian and Balkan affairs left Gaul open to invasion. Partly because his defence policy proved costly to the senatorial class. But most of all, perhaps, because to the Romans he signified the arrival of Arianism. That the identification of Goths and

Vandals with this form of Christianity should have seemed so natural, and so horrifying, to Western Catholics calls for some explanation; for upon it depends, very largely, the history of the barbarian settlement of the West.

The Goths had learned their Christianity from a Greek named Ulfilas. For seven years (341–348) he had preached among them, and further, had translated the scriptures into their own tongue. But he was an Arian—that is to say, an exponent of the heresy ascribed to Arius, a believer in the divinity of the Father but not of the Son. It followed that the Goths, and their neighbours the Vandals, were also Arians. One may easily enough dismiss the fierce opposition of the Western Catholics—strict disciples of Augustinian theology— as the natural reaction of an established church, that had fought hard to survive, to an interloper. Like the great Roman land-owners, the Western church had property to lose, and intended not to. All this must never be lost sight of. And yet, behind it, in the full doctrine of the Trinity, lay the very heart of historical Christianity. Blood and language held Roman and barbarian far apart; but these gaps were easily bridgeable as compared with the gap in belief.

Alaric, therefore, was the chieftain of an Arian race; and when, in 410, he finally took Rome, it was not to be expected that his comparatively restrained behaviour in the City of St. Peter would earn him many good marks from Western writers. He ought to have sacked Rome, and hence it was believed that he did. In truth, however, he cannot have had much interest in the place, once it had fallen, for the desperate need of his people was for food rather than for plunder; and, as St. Jerome remarked, there was none in Rome.

Where was food to be had? Scarcely in Italy, where the produce of the countryside could not even suffice to feed the bigger towns. The Roman population had been supplied with corn and oil from the province of Africa—and the Count of Africa had not hesitated to cease shipments when he heard that the Visigoths were investing Rome. Blockade was the trump card in the hand of the Emperors so long as they controlled Africa and the sea. The Visigoths tried to reach Africa, always the barbarian goal, but failed. Retreat from Italy along the Mediterranean coast was the only remaining course, the Balkan route being blocked by yet more barbarians. And the Goths took it.

Tribes in search of food and food-producing lands move swiftly. They might be thought to take small notice of sitting tenants' rights, and just as little of each other's. But yet, in the course of a mere generation or two, the Germanic peoples had settled down among the Romans on the Western lands that were, in general, to be their permanent homes; in Africa, reached after an incredible migration through Gaul and Spain, the Vandals; in Spain and Southern Gaul, the Visigoths; in Northern Gaul, the Franks; in Eastern Gaul, the Burgundians; in Italy, successors to the Visigoths, the Ostrogoths.

The relationship of these settlers with the established population, their assumptions about Roman rule and their attitude towards the civilization they found, conformed in general to a single pattern. This we know not only from written records (all Roman or romanized) but also from archaeology and from the study of place-names and linguistic forms.

That the barbarians should have taken the best agricultural land was to have been expected. What might seem less obvious was their apparent eagerness to take account, so far as they could understand it, of the complexities of local tenurial practice. Even when they chose to live together in exclusive Germanic communities, they took notice of the ways of those they supplanted. One explanation of this may lie in the comparative smallness of their numbers. For the most part they were landlords, not labourers; farmers, not slaves; and their desire was to live upon the countryside in the most profitable, that is, the best-tried, way. The Roman system of agriculture remained unaffected for the simple reason that it was the fruit not of political contrivance but of intelligent submission, over the years, to the limitations imposed by soil and climate. Improvement in agricultural technique could alone bring about serious modification; and it was not easy to improve on Rome. In Gaul, Spain and Italy we can observe the same intricate process of land-redistribution; barbarians taking over estates, or fractions of them, anxiously determining their boundaries, learning how best to exploit the arable, carefully observing the rights of property; in short, behaving as *hospites*, guests of the Roman world. This was no elaborate pretence. As their ancestors before them, the new barbarians had come, though in far greater numbers, to enjoy the Roman lands; and the fact that their swords were drawn in no way diminished their resolve to behave like Romans. After all, they were old acquaintances. This is why Gothic place-names in Southern Gaul so often contain a personal and so seldom a Gothic topographical element (e.g. brook, wood); for the Goths knew their Romans well and thus understood topographical terms of Latin origin. To tighten their dependence upon Western traditions and their allegiance to the Emperors was their cherished hope. Perhaps this retarded the already far-developed process of differentiation between the parts of the Empire they occupied. (Students of Late Latin are satisfied that the basic distinctions between French, Spanish and Italian are pre-barbarian.)

Within this common framework of consent there are divergencies and difficulties to be noted. And, first, in the Visigothic lands.

Despite their numbers—there may have been as many as 100,000 warriors in Aquitaine—the Visigoths seem to have been unable, and perhaps unwilling, to resist the drift towards romanization. We must not be deceived by the reported boast of their chieftain, Athaulf, that he had once considered turning *Romania* into *Gothia* but had then thought better of it. These are reported words. The fact was that the Goths, as a separate people, might very soon have ceased to exist had they not also been Arians. For example, their legal remains demonstrate how their customary way of life became at once, and heavily, influenced by Roman usage. Intermarriage, again, was bound to dilute not their blood only but also their language. For many Goths of the second and succeeding generations, Latin was the mother-tongue.

In the course of the fifth century, Aquitaine, Gascony, Narbonne, Provence and the greater part of Spain fell under Gothic tutelage. Are we to conceive this as planned expansion?

The first Gothic incursion into Southern Gaul was in search of food. Athaulf had informed the Emperor that hostilities must start once more because grain had not been

provided, as promised, for his people; and famine obliged him
to move once more, from Gaul into Spain. The imperial fleets
had established an effective blockade, and the Mediterranean
ports were kept clear of barbarians for so long as it was humanly
possible. The Goths could settle on the Atlantic seaboard if
they wished, and could quarter themselves upon the inland
farms of Aquitaine; Britain, equally, and the Northern provinces
of the Empire could be abandoned to other barbarians, if need
be; but the great Mediterranean ports of Gaul and Spain must
be held at any cost. Upon this, almost alone, the Eastern and
Western Emperors were agreed, and were prepared to co-
operate. It becomes clear, therefore, that the great areas of land
covered by the ranging Goths had attracted them for no other
reason than that the lands they left behind them were always
insufficient to ward off starvation. With Africa's supplies cut off,
the Roman West could barely feed itself, let alone the new-
comers.

One may contrast, perhaps, the attitudes of two sorts of
Romans to the Goths, mobile despite themselves: the landed
proprietors in their midst, and the officials responsible for
keeping them out of forbidden zones.

Of the landed proprietors, one, a victim of dispossession,
left an elaborate record of his experiences. Paulinus of Pella, a
Gallo-Roman nobleman, had had Goths billetted on his estates
near Bordeaux. Pillage and political miscalculation combined
to rob him of all his possessions; and so he fled to Marseilles,
and there learned what it meant to live in straitened circumstances. Only one bit of good luck came his way: an unknown
Goth, he writes, "wishing to buy a certain small property that
had once been mine, actually sent me the price of it—not, of
course, a price representing anything like its true value—but I
confess I received it as a gift from heaven; for it enabled me to
build up somewhat the shreds of my scattered fortune and even
to ward off, a little, the kind of comment that wounds me."
Paulinus was a Catholic.

As for the Roman officials, none in the West was greater
than the Patrician Aetius, effective master of Italy and Gaul. His
task was to defend Gaul from complete barbarian absorption:
it was threatened from all sides. This he achieved, over the

years, by playing off chieftain against chieftain and people
against people. High-minded loyalty to the Empire is not,
however, the impression of his motives that contemporaries
seem to have obtained. (He once voluntarily surrendered a
province of the Empire to the barbarians.) He was a great landowner, a dynast with enemies at court, a man who could never
afford to be disinterested; and hence public and private issues
were deeply entwined in every one of his decisions. He was
what, in the Middle Ages, historians would call a feudal magnate of the first rank, a great marcher lord with interests everywhere. To save Eastern Gaul from the Burgundians, Aetius
called in the Huns from central Europe, where they now stood
poised between the two Empires; and the Huns effectively
reduced the Burgundians to manageable dimensions, the
manner in which this was done becoming a main theme of
bardic recitation. The Huns were also employed against the
Visigoths, who had taken advantage of Roman pre-occupation
in the North to strengthen their own hold over the South.
The Goths of Toulouse, besieged by a Hun contingent under a
Roman general, not only held out but captured and executed
the general. This was in 439. There was nothing here to suggest
that the Gallo-Roman aristocracy had accepted the *fait accompli*
of Gothic *condominium*. They were prepared to fight on—and,
what is more serious, to fight on with auxiliaries compared
with whom the Goths were simple gentleman-farmers. The
conclusion, difficult to resist, that Aetius was interested chiefly
in saving the landed wealth of his own family and his own
class, at whatever cost, is further supported by his employment
of the Huns in Western Gaul, where they were called upon
to put down a major rising of exasperated peasants and slaves.[1]
This rising was a very serious matter, involving the whole of
Western Gaul, and its causes lay deep in the past, among years
of maladministration, extortion and neglect. Yet the answer
of Aetius, when the storm broke, was simple repression; and
the Huns were his instrument.

[1]Probably to this period belong the occasional Hunnic settlements in
Gaul, e.g. the village of Pont-l'Abbé near Quimper in Brittany, the inhabitants of which still retain the characteristic Hunnic skull, quite distinct from
that of any Germanic people.

In 451 the Huns under Attila, their greatest warrior, turned on their former employers and invaded Gaul in force, ostensibly to attack the Visigothic kingdom of Toulouse. The threat was sufficient to draw Aetius and the Visigoths together; and so, in the summer, side by side, they faced Attila on the Catalaunian Plains, near Troyes, and defeated him. Attila was thrown out of Gaul; and his next, and last, blow—to Aetius' consternation —was to fall upon Italy. The point, however, that matters is that the defeat might well have been a rout and the harrying of Italy might never have happened if Aetius had so chosen; for he held back the Visigoths from their final charge, preferring, as it appears, that the Huns should survive to fight for him another day, presumably against the Visigoths. Aetius was the last Roman of the West who stood—and fought—for anything remotely resembling an imperial interest (though this did not, in fact, save him from the Emperor Valentinian III's dagger). He fought with barbarians against barbarians; his interests were those of a narrow senatorial order, in whose hands still lay the best properties not taken over by the barbarians. One of his dearest hopes, the extinction of the Visigoths, was so far from being realized that the Visigothic kingdom reached its zenith some years after his murder; and yet, to contemporaries, there seemed to be something Roman about him, which, whatever it was, died with him.

The Goths and the Huns together succeeded in one piece of unplanned constructiveness for which they are seldom given credit. They gave new meaning to the Western church. This they achieved by causing bishops everywhere to be identified with local resistance; by attacking the City of Rome; and, in the case of the Goths, simply by being Arians.

Many biographical studies, some contemporary, tell us of the Gallo-Roman bishops' reactions to invasion. They constitute, naturally, a propaganda-literature that calls for careful handling. Yet there is no cause to doubt the substantial accuracy of their common contention—that the Catholic bishops rose to the occasion, adversity being the Christian's proper element. They led where the civil authorities failed. We have, for example, an Aquitanian poet's picture of an aged bishop leading his flock out of his burning city; another of St. Aignan heartening the citizens of Orleans; a third—this non-episcopal—of St. Genovefa persuading the Parisians not to flee. The impression left is that the bishops, and the Catholic communities in general, were for stability. They proposed to stay where they were, on their own property. The barbarians, after all, might prove not much more objectionable than the officials, by turns negligent and extortionate, of the imperial government in Ravenna. This, perhaps, accounts for the curious double theme of Aquitanian Christian literature: on the one hand, the Goths were welcomed as saviours from the Romans, and on the other attacked for their ruthless treatment of church property and, more significantly, of Catholic leaders. It took the Goths some time to appreciate the value of the Catholic bishops as intermediaries between themselves and the imperial government, though, even where they did, they held themselves aloof as Arians. Nevertheless, the Catholic communities of Roman Gaul may be said to have triumphed merely by surviving; and it may be noted that except in Africa the Arians were everywhere far more tolerant of the Catholics than were the Catholics of the Arians. The Catholic bishops had become identified in men's minds with conservation, with continuity and with that very tradition of *Romanitas* that their predecessors had threatened. Moreover, they had done so without assistance. Gallicanism was born.

The attacks on Italy are similarly reflected in Christian biographies. We read that Maximus, bishop of Turin, vainly exhorted his flock not to fear the Huns and to have faith in God, who had permitted David to triumph over Goliath. Had it not been promised in the Scriptures that any town would be spared in which there were but ten just men? Turin was not spared. Still less was the great city of Aquileia of which, in the succeeding century, men found it hard to trace the site. And there were many others. But the greatest of all, Rome, was more fortunate. She suffered, of course, from more than one barbarian visitation; archaeologists have found evidence of destruction and burning within the walls. Yet substantially she remained as Antiquity had known her, till the middle of the sixth century. What was more important, the Bishops of Rome were beginning to achieve an effective primacy, not yet over

Europe but over Italy and the City itself. This was not inevitable. As we have seen, the senatorial order, the principal landowners of Italy, were at home and at their most powerful in Rome. Nor was their stranglehold upon territorial politics relaxed because, in the course of time, they had ceased to be pagan and had become Catholic. The Emperor, too, though absent, had his official representative among them. The predominance slowly achieved by the Bishops of Rome must be attributed to a variety of causes, the absence of any one of which might have proved fatal to them.

Among these causes may be distinguished, first, economic power. The bishopric of Rome had been richly endowed with land by the Emperor Constantine, and this endowment had grown steadily to that point where the bishops were wealthier than any senatorial family. Secondly, the bishops showed intelligence and aptitude in adapting imperial administrative traditions to their own uses; the earliest papal documents (dating from the late fourth century) derive from a chancery unmistakably modelled upon the Roman imperial chancery. Here was continuity of a sort well calculated, whether intentionally or not, to lull suspicion and to inspire confidence. Furthermore, the bishopric had its own library; and this went for something in a city of once-famous pagan libraries. Again, the Roman bishops developed and propagated that most potent of all medieval Christian cults, the cult of St. Peter, first Bishop of Rome. The primacy, implied in this claim, over all other sees was never allowed to go by default; the successors of St. Peter, bishop and martyr, spoke with a special prestige simply because they were his successors. Added to this was their alacrity in championing the full Trinitarian doctrine of St. Augustine and the African Fathers in the face of Germanic Arianism. They stood for orthodoxy. Finally, like many other bishops, they showed to best advantage in—and, it is not unfair to add, made the most of—political adversity. They proved themselves natural leaders; and Catholic apologists did not allow men to forget it. Thus, circumstances conspired to exalt the bishopric of Rome from the comparative obscurity of the early fourth century to the notoriety of the early fifth.

In the summer of the year 452, Attila's Huns paused, in

their southward advance through Italy, near Mantua. Here they were met by an embassy comprising, we must suppose, the three most influential Romans of their time, men whose imperial commission was backed by the full authority of the senate. One of the three was Pope Leo I. His ecclesiastical pre-eminence may have meant little enough to the pagan Attila; but to the Romans he must have seemed the natural mouth-piece of the Emperor, an official whose predecessors had bar-gained with Goths for the preservation of the City and whose landed wealth ensured direct interest in keeping the new barbarians on the move. No eye-witness account survives of the interview. It may not have contributed very materially to Attila's decision to make peace and retreat north into the Hunnic domains of Central Europe. We know that plague and famine were decimating his forces. But future generations of Romans did not fail to associate the Pope's name with the deliverance of their city from the Huns.

An obvious but remarkable feature of the Western Empire's collapse before the barbarians was the anxiety of Romans and barbarians alike to cling to the ancient forms of political life. With their military power in commission, their administration in shreds and their thoughts largely bound up with insoluble dynastic problems, the last Western Emperors, stranded in Ravenna, seemed to their contemporaries not less significant than the Emperors of Antiquity. Their name and title remained associated with that most characteristic imperial function, the giving of law. A mere twelve years before the irruption of Attila, the Emperor Theodosius II issued his great codex, or collection of imperial decrees and letters, to be equally valid in Ravenna and in Constantinople. The historical study of this mighty collection is still in its infancy, and in any case this is not the place to consider its details; but it must be emphasized that nothing could have been better calculated to demonstrate the vigour of the imperial office in what was probably its most important function. Not that the codex was designed simply to impress by its bulk; it was for the use of lawyers and students and was arranged, with this in view, in sixteen sections, of which the last (*de fide catholica*) was concerned with the doctrine and organization of the Catholic church. This collection dominated the legal, and therefore political, thinking of Western Europe throughout the early Middle Ages, and was only gradually replaced, and then not universally, by the later collection of the Emperor Justinian. What is more, it at once, and vitally, affected the ways in which the new barbarian kingdoms thought about themselves and their relationship with Rome. Apart from three main statements of barbarized Roman Law (Ostrogothic, Burgundian and Visigothic) intended primarily for the use of Romans living under barbarian rule, the barbarians drew heavily upon the lawbooks of Theodosius when they came to set down in writing their own customs. For example, the surviving portions of the laws of the Visigoth Euric (464) are so deeply impregnated with Roman Law that one begins to wonder whether any hard and fast distinction should ever be drawn between Roman and barbarian law: all *law*, it might be argued, was for Europe, Roman *ex hypothesi*.

Prestige, however, could not save the young Emperor Romulus Augustulus from deposition by the barbarians in 476; and he proved to be—what no one could have foreseen—the last of the Western Emperors. Many an Emperor had met with a violent end; many had owed their thrones to the support of an army or a clique of powerful men; but none, before, had been without a successor. The Eastern Emperor, Zeno, was politely informed that there was no immediate need for his Western colleague: the barbarians would prefer to place themselves directly under his aegis. In a sense, of course, this was to say no more than the Popes had been saying for some time—that the Roman Empire, like the Roman Church, was indivisible. Yet, even so, the chroniclers of the time show an awareness that something bigger had happened. One of them writes, "and so the Western Empire of the Roman people perished with this Augustulus—and from now the Gothic kings possessed Rome and Italy".

Augustulus (it was a derisive nickname) lost his throne, though not his life, because he and those who sheltered behind him were unable to satisfy the needs of the mixed barbarian hordes in Northern Italy for lands and for food. He protected, in short, the landed interest—the interest of senate and church and great families which, united, had been second only to the barbarian settlers themselves as a formative influence on Late Roman politics. The chieftain to whom the work of deposition fell was a Hun named Odoacer; and we must assume that a part of his following was also Hun. This, more than anything, will explain the loathing in which most Romans held him and the pleasure they took in magnifying his eventual downfall at the hands of a Goth. He belonged to the terrible people; the people who, the Romans chose to believe, slew and ate their old men, drank blood and slept on horseback; the people whose wonderful barbaric lament over the corpse of their hero, Attila, conserves something of its fire even in the Latin guise in which we have it. The support of a few Roman families and the seeming neutrality of the papacy should not blind us to Odoacer's unpopularity. How could it be otherwise with a man branded tyrant in Byzantium? His overthrow was implicit, not in the nature of his twelve years' rule in Italy (of which almost nothing is known), but in his failure to obtain official recognition. He died as he had lived, the chieftain of the clans settled on the estates of the Po valley. We must not be deceived by titles and juridical forms.

Odoacer's conqueror was an Ostrogothic warrior named Theodoric, who had marched his people from the East into Italy with full imperial approval, to dispossess the Huns and their allies of their estates and of anything else that was theirs. Once again, Huns and Goths were let loose on one another, and the total disappearance of the former suggests something of the merciless savagery of barbarian warfare in the heroic age. Tradition asserted that Theodoric slew Odoacer with his own hand. Men wished to believe it. To us, it is of more interest that Theodoric and his Goths, though Arians, were at once accepted by the Roman senate and people. It was the senate, the official landowning class, that ruined Odoacer and made possible the reign of Theodoric—and this not because Theodoric either could or did rule in a manner unlike Odoacer. He was sent by the Emperor. That was enough. Here, as throughout all the difficult days of the dissolution of Antiquity, we can trace the hard, selfish interest of a comparatively small group of families, their wealth and influence founded upon land. No stronger stabilizing influence can be imagined than the determination of these families to preserve their heritage intact, and to acknowledge no lord but the Roman Emperor.

The Ostrogoths settled, as a people, upon the estates in the Po valley farmed by their predecessors before them. Place-name study confirms this; but it would be making too tidy a picture to deny that many Goths made their homes south of this area. In fact, the impression is that Theodoric did not bunch the greater part of his people in the Po valley for fear of the Romans but rather because the danger that threatened him was from the North. Barbarians who were able to establish themselves further South, in isolated communities, were unmolested by the Romans. In general, however, the Goths took over the lands vacated by the mixed tribes owing allegiance to Odoacer, and went to some pains to avoid clashes with the interests of the landed aristocracy of Rome, lay and clerical alike. Theodoric seems even to have appointed a Roman to act as arbitrator in the assignment of properties.

As lord of his own subjects and the acknowledged representative of the Emperor, Theodoric enjoyed complete control of Italy. His problem was not to evolve subtle plans for fusion and unification but to rule both Goths and Romans as they found themselves upon the land, and to protect both from the threat of further barbarian peoples in search of food. In effect, this meant that the Roman administration of Italy continued as before; and, inasmuch as he had an imperial commission, Theodoric was accorded full honours by the senate and the people of Rome. Italy's crisis was not therefore constitutional but political and, more specifically, tenurial. But that there was a crisis was implicit in every line of the extraordinary literature to which Theodoric's settlement gave rise.

It was to have been expected that the Roman officials whose work brought them most in touch with the barbarian king would give what emphasis they could to the orthodoxy of his rule. But we are faced with something more—something without precedent in the annals of Roman-barbarian co-operation: a deliberate effort, on the part of the Romans, to represent Theodoric as a greater barbarian than in fact he was. The leader of this enterprise was Cassiodorus, a Roman senator of rare distinction and learning, whose special achievement

was to provide Theodoric with a false genealogy connecting
him with the family of Ermanaric the Amal, the greatest of the
Gothic chieftains of the days before the Hunnic avalanche.[1]
In truth, Theodoric was something of a parvenu, as every other
Goth must have been aware. He owed his position not to blood
and ancestry but to successful leadership in battle. This being
the case, the Gothic lords of Italy were unlikely to be impressed
by the work of Cassiodorus. Recent research tends to cast
doubt upon the traditional view that the Germans cared, above
all else, that their chieftains should belong to the right dynasties; chieftains owed their power to their own right arms, and
handed it on to their children if they could. Who, then, but
the Romans themselves stood to be impressed by Theodoric
the Amal? Should we not interpret the work of Cassiodorus in
the light of the devouring interest of the great Roman houses
in all that pertained to genealogy? This it was that made
Theodoric respectable.

But Cassiodorus did more than reconcile his friends with
the new barbarians. He engaged actively in the great undertaking of preserving the writings of Antiquity for the future.
It must again be emphasized that the Roman aristocrats of the
period saw clearly that they were heirs to a highly complex
legacy. Literature, law and religion were its inseparable elements, just as they had been in the days of St. Ambrose and
Symmachus (whose family was still active in Rome). Paganism,
naturally, was no longer a political force, though it lingered in
many surprising corners. Christianity had supplanted it. And
just as the senators had once striven in the face of imperial
opposition to preserve their religious rites as the dearest part
of their heritage, so now they stood for the full Catholic tradition
of St. Augustine, or at least for as much of it as they could
assimilate. This was why they looked on the Pope as one of
themselves. It was only to be expected, therefore, that men like
Cassiodorus and Boethius should think of their work for
secular learning in terms of the heritage of Catholic Christendom. As Cassiodorus, in retirement at Vivarium, where he and
his disciples observed a variant of St. Benedict's Rule, gathered

[1]Ermanaric's own name was omitted, perhaps because he was known to
have committed suicide.

about him the manuscripts of Roman law and letters, and as Boethius embarked on his tremendous (and unfinished) task of translating into Latin the complete works of Plato and Aristotle as they reached him from Africa and Byzantium, each was inspired to make available to the Romano-Catholic community the full heritage of the past. No trace of Christianity will be found in Boethius' famous prison-dialogue 'On the Consolation of Philosophy'; scholars have searched for it often enough. But the same pen wrote the theological tractates, 'On the Trinity', 'On the Catholic Faith' and 'Against Eutyches'. Cassiodorus, to whom Cicero and St. Augustine were almost equally dear, divided that most influential of educational manuals, his 'Institutions', into two parts—of divine and of secular letters; and the divine took precedence.[1] The opening words of his preface express his sadness that, while there were plenty of scholars ready to teach secular letters, there were few to teach the divine scriptures. That had to be put right.

Why the sense of urgency? Because the Ostrogoths were Arians. Nothing, no amount of compromise on inessential points or courtesy to the successor of St. Peter, could conceal this basic fact, upon which Theodoric's kingdom—like that of every other Arian chieftain—ultimately foundered. Arianism was the foe that brought papacy and aristocracy together and made of both the loyal subjects of Byzantium. The prosperity of Italy under Gothic rule could hide the real danger only so long as no major issue of principle was raised.

The crisis, as it turned out, was of Byzantine making. The Emperor Justin succeeded in clearing up certain doctrinal issues that had estranged his predecessors from Rome and then, in 523, issued a law, valid in Italy, excluding pagans, Jews and heretics—by which he meant Arians—from public employment. Whether this law was aimed at Theodoric is not known; but the Goths certainly reacted as if it had been, and Theodoric's last years were marked by his persecution of Catholics. Boethius was only one of his victims. It is essential not to regard this sudden turn of events as unforeseen. Catholics and

---

[1]Influential, but not necessarily as a textbook. In many monastic and episcopal schools it was rather a book of reference, like Isidore's 'Etymologiae' and the 'Nuptiae' of Martianus Capella.

Arians were quite used to persecuting each other, and there is plenty of evidence of friction between the two in Italy through-out the period of Ostrogothic occupation. An instance of this was the anger of the Romans at the destruction by the Goths of a Catholic church at the gates of Verona, when there could not have been much doubt that the intention was simply to make possible the completion of the town's fortifications. Pope John I made no attempt to conceal his hostility to the Arians, and his death in a Gothic prison caused him to be honoured as a Catholic martyr. Theodoric, dying not long after, was held to be the victim of divine justice.

Theodoric's signal misfortune was that he had no son to succeed him. He was one of the few barbarian lords whose achievements were such that he might well have founded a dynasty. His daughter he married to a Visigoth, otherwise obscure, whose distinction was that the blood of Ermanaric really did run in his veins. But he died before his father-in-law, leaving his wife to manage the Goths as best she could. Dis-integration was bound to follow.

It is sometimes stated that Theodoric envisaged himself as head of a Germanic federation of Europe. This was not the case. But there can be no question that he interested himself actively in the affairs of Frankish Gaul, Visigothic Spain and Vandal Africa; not least, because he was afraid of them. The early years of his rule were devoted to the prosecution of Gothic claims in Illyricum and Pannonia, the Balkan lands through which he had once passed and in which the master of Italy could never afford to be disinterested. And then, in 507, his thoughts turned West. The result was a series of dynastic marriages which bound his family to the families of other barbarian kings. What did he hope to gain by this? Security, it seems probable, against the intrigues of the Emperor with the Franks in Gaul. The withdrawal of imperial authority and its transference to the Frankish king could ruin the Ostrogothic kingdom overnight. Hence Theodoric's concern to interest the Burgundians, the Vandals and the Visigoths in the affairs of his house.[1] Hence, also, his particular touchiness about the

[1]Ostrogothic coins found North of the Alps bear witness to commercial contacts.

rich, exposed lands of Provence that linked him with Visigothic Septimania. Cassiodorus has preserved for us some of
the extraordinary diplomatic correspondence that passed
between Theodoric and his neighbours during this period.
From it emerges one unquestionable conclusion; the stability
of the Western Mediterranean lands depended, in increasing
measure, upon events in Northern Gaul. Considerations of
geography made this inevitable. Theodoric saw, as clearly as
some of his Roman and barbarian predecessors in Italy had
seen, that he could never afford to ignore Gaul. His marriage-
alliances, skilful though they were, had no deeper significance
than a plain resolve to keep the Franks out of the Mediterranean
world. European history in the succeeding centuries is largely
conditioned by their penetration into it.

We have, lastly, to consider the effect upon Europe of the
Vandal conquest of Roman Africa. From the first days of their
arrival in the West, the barbarians had made instinctively for
Africa; it was the granary of Europe and therefore Mecca to
the hungry, uprooted Germans. If Alaric had had the ships to
get there his successor would not have marched out of Italy
into Southern Gaul. Eastern and Western Emperors were at
least agreed on the absolute necessity of denying Mediterranean
ports and shipping, and even knowledge of ship-building, to
the barbarians for as long as possible. An edict of 419 punished
with death certain Romans who had taught the secrets of
ship-building to the Vandals. But it was too late. Within a
few years the Vandals had made the crossing from Spain to
Africa.

The Vandals in Africa acquired an importance out of all
proportion to their numbers, and this despite the fact that they
were not a united people. We may attribute this importance to
three factors. First, the Vandals were sitting upon Europe's
life-line, and could (and did) cut off supplies of corn and oil
at will; secondly, they were among the fiercest of the Arians,
just as the Africans were among the fiercest of the Catholics;
and thirdly, they were masters of the province with the best
claims to be considered the intellectual centre of the Roman
world. We may add, if we wish, that they were ruled at the
most critical period by a chieftain of exceptional ability,

Geiseric. One historian has even called him the subtlest statesman of his century.

Information about the Vandal invasion is relatively plentiful by reason of the stir it caused in the African Church. The
African bishops, like their European colleagues, suddenly
found themselves leaders of local resistance against a ruthless
enemy. Some, St. Augustine among them, stood firm. Others
fled, with or without their flocks. A few even became Arians.
It may easily be appreciated that the wealthy Africans had
more reason than most to seek a basis of agreement with the
invaders; vast fortunes were at stake. Corruption and compromise went hand in hand. Where this failed, persecution
began—a persecution more savage and, in one sense, more
eagerly courted than anywhere in the West. When their turn
came, the Catholics proved equally relentless. For a while,
the Emperors were powerless to intervene. They watched the
Vandal advance along the coast from city to city, the destruction
of much of the wealth of the great province and the decimation
of the Catholic Church. They watched Rome starve and the
Vandals raiding the Italian coast without hindrance. Constantinople felt also the constriction of Mediterranean trade. Indeed,
it seems probable that Mediterranean economy never recovered
from the chaos into which it was then thrown. East and West
were not, of course, entirely cut off from one another, nor is it
true that goods were no longer reaching Europe from Africa
and the Levant; but the contacts were spasmodic, the confidence of the merchant class had been shaken; new markets
were sought. Fear of what this might lead to must have been a
decisive factor in moving the Eastern Emperors to help their
Western colleagues and, when they had none, to intervene
alone to restore imperial power in the Western Mediterranean.
But another, not less important factor was religion. The Eastern
Emperors, in particular, were deeply involved in a religious
settlement which made of them, whether they wished it or not,
theologians and theocrats. Not to have heard the cry of Catholic
Africa and Catholic Italy would have been tantamount to a
renunciation of a basic imperial function, implicit not simply
in the work of Constantine but in that of Augustus himself.
With such interests at heart, Constantinople sent forces under

her best general, the barbarian Aspar, to assist the westerners to hold what remained of Roman Africa against the Vandals, and, after the withdrawal of the westerners, to fight on alone, and vainly. A second time, in 440, a great naval expedition left Constantinople to recapture Carthage, the capital city of the province—and this when Constantinople herself was gravely threatened by the Huns. It is a measure, therefore, of the vital importance attached by the Eastern Romans to Africa. Neither of these expeditions was successful. Still less were those planned by the West alone. It fell to the Emperor Justinian to plan and carry into effect what has come to be known as the Reconquest.

Justinian was by birth an Illyrian, a Latin-speaker. From this, scholars have sometimes inferred that he felt a degree of sympathy for Western affairs that a Greek-speaking Emperor would not have felt. There is little to support such a view. Justinian's most striking characteristic was an extreme orthodoxy of mind that led him to act as nearly as possible as he believed his predecessors would have acted. His concern for the West—at the expense, even, of an Eastern frontier constantly threatened by the Persian Empire—derived not from his blood but from an accurate diagnosis of imperial duty and interest. To represent the Reconquest as crude and useless archaism is utterly to misconceive the interests of sixth-century Byzantium. Its failure lay not in its conception but in its fearful cost and destructiveness.

A Greek, Procopius, with access to court circles, left a detailed account of Justinian's three great wars (the Persian, the Vandal and the Gothic) which, in conjunction with his mighty recodification of Roman Law, entitles him to be deemed the greatest and the most orthodox of the later Emperors. Of the two wars that comprised the Reconquest, both, Procopius wished his readers to understand, were embarked upon at the earnest wish of the enslaved Romans of the West. Repeated disappointments had not dulled their longing for liberation from Arian Vandals and Goths. The decision to invade, when it was finally taken, was based rather more on religious grounds than on the advice of the generals, some of whom told the Emperor that no attack on Africa could succeed without bases in Sicily and Italy. However, Belisarius was persuaded to lead the venture.

The collapse of Vandal Africa was swift. If we are to believe our sources, a large proportion of the Roman population welcomed their liberators, provided them with supplies and opened their towns to them. But it was on the battlefield that the Vandals were finally defeated.

Two interesting points emerge from the subsequent Roman resettlement of Africa. First, that the merchants seem not to have been too eager to return to traditional trade-routes; Justinian never quite succeeded in cajoling the Mediterranean world into believing that the Vandals had been a mere interlude. His resettlement of agricultural property and restoration of estates to the heirs of dispossessed Romans proved a good deal more successful than his mercantile policy. But, secondly, his religious resettlement exceeded the wildest hopes of the African Church, which not only received back its stolen properties but was given (and took) the chance to persecute the Arian hierarchy. Here is part of the message sent by the African clergy to Pope John II on the occasion of their first reunion in council at Carthage, in 534:

"We desire to resume the excellent customs of the past, suppressed during a century of tyranny and captivity despite unanimous protests. And so we are re-united in a synod of all Africa, in Justinian's basilica at Carthage—We leave your Holiness to guess how our tears of joy flow in such a place."

Almost without pausing, Justinian proceeded to the logical consequence of his victory. He undertook the re-establishment of imperial authority over Italy. But here the problem was more difficult, for barbarian rule had been milder, and Arian persecution less severe, than anything the Africans had known. It followed, therefore, that Roman Italy's welcome to the imperial forces might be less whole-hearted. Further, the Italians lacked that sense of provincial cohesion and pride that made it possible for the Africans to think and act unitedly. But, above all, the imperial commanders miscalculated the strength and intelligence of the Ostrogoths. The Italian war took not one season but twenty years to conclude; and in that time Italy was ravaged from end to end and her cities sacked as they had never been before. Much of the damage must be ascribed to the ferocity of the imperial mercenaries, who had less reason than the established Goths to protect the rights of property. Metropolitan Italy, and Rome herself, received a blow from which they never completely recovered. All the same, part of the disaster was due to natural causes, notably famine and plague, over which the armies had little or no control. Had the reconquest of Italy been accomplished with the same speed as the reconquest of Africa, there can be no serious question that Justinian would have been welcomed as a liberator. But a generation of campaigning and destruction precluded this. Italian separatism, anti-Greek feeling and local interests combined to assure the imperial troops a very meagre welcome when Rome finally fell.

No epic poet celebrated the reconquest of Italy.

At a prohibitive cost in blood and treasure, Justinian achieved the objective of his predecessors—the re-establishment of a Roman world skirting the Mediterranean. African, Italian and even Spanish ports were safe once more for Roman shipping. Whether, left in peace, this world could have resumed its ancient prosperity it is impossible to say; within a very short time Lombards and Arabs were to annul the Reconquest. But Justinian believed that it could; and there are signs of recovery, in Italy particularly, in the few short years of imperial rule, which hint at the correctness of that belief.

The constant factor in the years of disintegration at which we have been looking was the firm resolve of the Roman Emperors to restore *Romania*.

CHAPTER III

ITALY AND THE LOMBARDS

JUSTINIAN'S renewed rule over Western Europe was very soon put to the test; for Italy was almost at once invaded and in part occupied by the Lombards. It is important to appreciate the resolution and intelligence with which, over two centuries, the Eastern Emperors tried to defend that hard-won province, and the narrowness of the margin by which they failed.

We should know comparatively little about the Lombards in Italy, and infinitely less about their earlier history, were it not that one of them—Paul the Deacon, son of Warnefrid—decided to follow the example of Jordanes, and write, as a Roman would, a prose account of his people's exploits. And so it is proper to consider him first.

It need hardly be said that, in common with the other 'national' historians of the period, Paul, for all his virile pride in blood, thought of the past in terms of a developing Christian pattern; his people, once pagan and then Arian, were at last (though only just) Catholic. The victory of Catholicism, not the victory of the Lombards, is his theme. Paul himself was brought up at Pavia in the court of King Ratchis. In 775 or shortly afterwards he became a monk at Monte Cassino, professing St. Benedict's Rule, and remained there till, seven years later, family business took him North to the court of the greatest of all the barbarians, Charlemagne. He seems to have lived a good deal at Metz, the ancestral home of the Carolingian family. He wrote much and variously. In a small but influential book on the Bishops of Metz he took the opportunity (it may have been the real occasion of his writing) to recount the early history of Charlemagne's ancestors and notably of Bishop Arnulf. He wrote simply, with learning and vigour—qualities for which the Carolingians could always find a use; and it was only after a stay of some five years in the North that he felt free to return home to Monte Cassino. Once back, he continued his literary work. This included a Homiliary, much prized in the Frankish dominions (of which we still have no critical edition), and a History of the Lombards from the time when they first set out from the Baltic coast to the year of King Liutprand's death (744). Had he lived longer, Paul might have chosen to continue the story, somewhat after the manner of Gregory of Tours, for he had stopped at the point when, for him, contemporary history began. But, for all his diverse interests, his passion was for the past and in particular for the impact upon his barbarian ancestors of Rome and Christianity. He wrote a résumé of Roman History, carelessly enough put together, but vital to us as an indication of what really stirred the imaginations of barbarians in the eighth century.

Paul's Lombard History was immensely popular. It survives in many manuscripts. Why? Not because it gave to educated Lombards a more detailed or more vivid picture of their legendary past than they could have obtained from oral tradition and the songs of their own bards (of which Paul made use), and not because it soothed them in the moment of Lombard capitulation to Charlemagne, but because it showed them to themselves in a Roman mirror. The very actions of reading and writing history were Roman; to conceive of themselves in an historical context was Roman; to be Catholic was to be Roman. Our own difficulty is less to see the picture they saw in that mirror than to remember that the mirror is there at all.

Paul's account of the Lombard migration is not much more than a thumb-nail sketch, and time can easily be wasted in fruitless discussion of his sources. His general sketch of the movement from Scandinavia down through Central Europe to Pannonia does not entirely lack confirmation, though his details fall into the literary pattern set by Cassiodorus and Jordanes for the Ostrogothic migration. But this need not disturb us: the migrant German tribes had followed much the same course, and their experiences had become interchangeable for story-telling purposes. Long before Paul's time, there existed an accepted corpus of Germanic migration-legends upon which all Germans drew, more or less at random.

Now Paul, though a Lombard writing for Lombards, had

no wish to whitewash his ancestors. Indeed, his purpose was to emphasize their savagery. This revealed itself in their vendettas with neighbouring tribes, which grew no less fierce as they moved by degrees into the orbit of Roman and of Christian influence. It had been in the course of their occupation of the open land between the rivers Theiss and Danube, about the year 500, that they first met with Arian missionaries and became superficially Christian. Under the ferocious Alboin and in alliance with the Asiatic Avars, they set upon the Gepids and destroyed them, taking much booty. Alboin's own share included Rosamund, the daughter of the slain Gepid chieftain, Cunimund, out of whose skull the Lombard made a goblet called, in his language, a *scala*. Avar pressure, love of and need for plunder to reward followers, and the unremitting problem of finding new lands for food, drove Alboin south into Italy. He retreated rather than advanced over the Alps. We have no means of estimating the size of his following nor of determining how many were true Lombards, but it is unlikely that it was as numerous as the Ostrogoths under Theodoric. A second respect in which the Lombards were inferior to the Ostrogoths was that they did not enter Italy as imperial *federati* or allies but as enemies. The Eastern Emperors never forgot this, and for two centuries did all in their power to uproot them. Lombard hatred of the imperial Greeks was the fruit of fear; their hold on Italy was always precarious.

The North Italian plains into which the Lombards descended early in 568 were less prosperous than those Theodoric had found. It is easy to exaggerate the extent of the devastation of any war, but the fact remains that Italy had been the scene of long and bitter fighting between Greeks and Goths and their mercenaries, fighting which had affected both countryside and cities. Consequently, the late sixth century was, for Italy, a period of chronic famine and plague. The Lombards accentuated but did not create the difficulty. Famine and plague, and the alleviation of these, are the unvarying background to the growth of the political and territorial power of the Papacy in Italy.

Historians are not yet agreed about the attitude of the Lombards to the inhabitants of Italy and to the lands they farmed. A good deal turns on the meaning of a single sentence in Book III, chapter 16, of Paul's History. One school argues that the Lombards had no reason to inflict wilful suffering upon the Italians or to deprive them of their possessions; and there is evidence that some big landlords retained their lands and simply paid dues to the Lombards as tributaries. On the other hand it is hard to believe that even the first generation of Lombard warlords would (or could) have been content to farm no more than the waste lands of the North upon which Rome had traditionally settled her German mercenaries. Although the Catholic hierarchy of Northern Italy was not wholly destroyed and the Roman landlords not wholly enslaved, Alboin's Lombards were suspicious of the Romans and kept apart from them in so far as this was possible. (One field in which segregation was from the first impossible was that of commerce.) Paul tells us that they brought their own wives and children with them, and the evidence available strongly suggests that the Lombards succeeded in keeping intact their racial independence and their language longer than did any other Germanic people settled upon Roman territory.

Their characteristic social unit in Italy was the *fara*, or group of families living on a war footing, established in some stronghold from which raids into neighbouring territory could be organized and to which plunder could be carried and divided out. No doubt the *farae*, pre-Italian in date, were modified by contact with the elaborate civilization of Italy; but their retention points to the Lombards' resolve not to abandon exploitation as the best means of preserving the family.[1] So late as the twelfth century it was possible to gloss the word *fara* as 'kindred'. In other words, the blood connections lying beneath the new shapes that hereditary possession of land brings to a society had not even then been lost sight of. Nor does archaeology contradict this picture. The earliest Lombard grave-goods in Italy are, as in Pannonia, purely Germanic, and closely resemble those of all other German peoples in their pagan state, the Ostrogoths included. They do not perhaps entitle

---

[1] The earliest settlements were probably based on the strongpoints (*castra*) captured from the Romans and Byzantines, as were the earliest Frankish settlements in *Belgica Secunda*.

us to speak of an independent Lombardic art, but they do show us a people still semi-nomadic, huddled together among the properties of the men whose civilization they were not yet able to emulate. In Bury's phrase, their minds were still in the forests of Germany.

That the situation and outlook of the Lombards changed rapidly in the years following the death of Alboin was due largely to the great pope, Gregory I, and to St. Benedict, Gregory's master. The joint contribution of these two men to the stabilization of barbarian Europe was overwhelming.

St. Benedict is known to us only through a short biography composed, about 45 years after Benedict's death, by Gregory. It constitutes the second book of Gregory's *Dialogues*. Naturally, one may argue that, with no supporting evidence, narrative of this kind could contain almost no historical truth. We can take it on trust or not, as we feel inclined. Scholars have been generally disposed to accept it.

Gregory says that Benedict was born of substantial parents, in the province of Nursia. We may infer that the year of his birth would have been about 480. He was educated in Rome. Like others of his generation, he felt called, while still a youth, to the ascetic life, which he practised first at Subiaco, not far from the ruins of Nero's palace, and, later, on the great height of Monte Cassino, hanging over the road from Rome to Naples. Whatever his personal wishes, he attracted to himself a large company of disciples; and it was for the guidance of such men (but not, as is sometimes said, at the bidding of any pope) that he finally set down in writing his plan for a communal life grounded on the fundamental principles of humility, charity, obedience, stability, poverty and faith in providence that he had always insisted that his companions should observe. They were not new principles, any more than monasticism was a new way of living. But their combination was Benedict's work. The great monk—like most of his early followers he was never a priest—was also a worker of miracles. These not only brought him fame in his own day but became, as it were, part of the stock-in-trade of his followers in succeeding centuries. Thaumaturgy and the cultivation of the miraculous were among the enduring interests of the Benedictines.

St. Benedict's Rule has survived in a copy, made at Aix for Charlemagne, of a version sent to him by Theodemar, abbot of Monte Cassino. This version was a direct copy of that of St. Benedict himself; and thus we have, in Charlemagne's copy, something which is probably unique in the field of antique texts—a copy only separated from the original by a single intermediary. We may therefore be reasonably certain that we know what St. Benedict wrote down.

This is not the place in which to examine the Rule in any detail. It bristles with textual problems. In our present context its main interest lies in its mere existence, standing as it does between Antiquity and the Middle Ages, drawing heavily upon the past, yet designed to meet the needs of a new, barbarian age. Even its language takes account of this; for St. Benedict wrote, not in the classical Latin he would have been taught in Rome, but in Vulgar Latin—the tongue spoken by his own contemporaries. His Rule was intended for use.

It was intended for use by cenobites; that is, by monks living according to a Rule and under a father or abbot, in a community to which a vow of stability tied them to the hour of death, and in a house which satisfied all their needs. To enter such a community was not necessarily easy. But this did not ultimately prevent the diffusion of communities following the Benedictine Rule, or some variant of it, all over Western Europe, thereby creating as well as solving social problems to which fuller reference must be made elsewhere in this book. St. Benedict defined with great skill the way in which his communities were to order themselves, and how they were to spend their time. He did not expect his monks to practise extreme asceticism like desert fathers, but rather to live disciplined lives in families, perhaps after the fashion of the best Roman families of the past, close to the soil and under the control of an abbot whose position was not entirely unlike that of the Roman *paterfamilias*, though that was not why he was called *Abbas*, 'father'.

The Rule divided the monk's day into properly balanced periods of manual labour, of study and of attendance at the divine offices. All three were conceived as parts of a spiritual whole, but it was the last that was its heart and purpose. The observance of a regular discipline was a means to an end, and never an end in itself. The discipline of a strictly ordered communal life made possible what was far harder to come by in the secular world—the uninterrupted offering up to God of praise, and of prayer for the salvation of souls, following the pattern evolved by the Roman Church and described in her laws. That communities of men might perform their rightful Christian duty with a singleness of purpose that diocesan clergy could seldom achieve was St. Benedict's whole object. But he would have trembled to hear that one day his monks, now learned and ordained, would become the rivals of the diocesan or secular clergy.

St. Benedict died at Monte Cassino in March, 547, or shortly afterwards; and there he was buried beside his sister, St. Scholastica. At the time of his death, three Italian communities were certainly following his Rule, and no doubt there were others. But thirty years later the Lombards swept through Italy, destroying all religious establishments. One monastery only—St. Mark's at Spoleto—is known to have survived in territory controlled by the Lombards. Some of the monks of Monte Cassino managed to escape the fury of the Lombard duke, Zotto, and reached Rome, bearing with them the autograph of their Rule. The papacy saved the work of St. Benedict and turned it to apostolic use.

A chief instrument in this act of conservation was Pope Gregory, known to posterity, though not to contemporaries, as the Great. Why his reputation did not stand higher in his own lifetime, and why the earliest biography of him is as slight as it is, is not at all obvious.[1] Yet the fact remains that the short notice of his career inserted in the late seventh century in the *Liber Pontificalis* (an invaluable semi-official series of papal biographies) bears little resemblance to the picture of him that his own writings afford, and still less to the picture that the medieval hagiographers (notably Englishmen) preferred to propagate. All that can be said with certainty is that

---

[1] It is the work of a contemporary of Bede, a monk of Whitby, who appears to have put together what shreds of information he could find in order that the result might be used in the course of the annual celebration of St. Gregory's day in his monastery.

this uncompromising pope stirred up an enmity against himself which is reflected in the timid notice of the *Liber Pontificalis* as well as in the later tradition that after his death the crowd wished to burn his library. Of Gregory's actual achievement, however, there can be no question. His deeds and writings speak for themselves and have no need of biographical assistance. They show us the first great pope of the Middle Ages, the disciple at once of St. Benedict and of St. Augustine.

Like St. Benedict, Gregory belonged to Rome. He was brought up there. But, unlike St. Benedict, he was much involved in Roman politics, being prefect of the city before renouncing secular life and turning his family estates in Sicily and on the Coelian Hill into houses of monks. This he did in the year 575, two years before the sack of Monte Cassino and three before the death of the aged Cassiodorus. From his Coelian house, dedicated to St. Andrew and following the Rule of St. Benedict, he was taken, early in 590, to become pope. His predecessor had died of the plague then ravaging Italy; and Paul, in his Lombard History, connects this plague with the flooding of the Tiber, down which a quantity of serpents, including an exceptionally fine dragon, were observed on their way to the sea. Gregory began his pontificate with a seven-fold litany of intercession, during the performance of which no less than eighty participants fell down dead. Without being too concerned about the details, we may recognize in this story the authentic setting for his pontificate. It was a time of utmost crisis, of plague, famine and devastation.

Gregory was not the first pope to face trials of this nature: the parallel with the pontificate of Leo the Great naturally suggested itself to contemporaries. He was not the first pope to have been schooled in the Roman tradition, nor to have served an important apprenticeship as a diplomat at Constantinople, nor to have meditated long upon the difficult writings of St. Augustine. But he was the first of the many disciples of St. Benedict to fill St. Peter's chair. His literary devotion to St. Benedict, implicit in the biography that is the second book of the *Dialogues*, caused the Byzantine Greeks to distinguish him from others of the same name by the title ὁ Διάλογος.

This biography, in the view of some scholars, had almost

as much to do with the immense popularity of the Rule as did its own merits. It forms part of a work originally, and more helpfully, called *The Miracles of the Italian Fathers*, but later known as the *Dialogues* by reason of the convention observed by the author. No pains were spared in seeking material for the book. The pope's correspondence contains several requests for information, and instances of his anxiety to interview old men whose memories might help him. He warns his readers against credulity, urging them to seek evidence for reported miracles, evidence, not so much that the miracles actually happened as that they were vouched for by men of high moral standing. Hagiographical evidence and historical evidence were never of the same order to the medieval mind. Gregory thus perhaps contributed as much as anyone to the establishing of that magnificent literary genre, medieval hagiography, the vast historical wealth of which is even now barely tapped. By miracles and by a new Christian mythology, the superstitious mind of the barbarian could be tempted and won.

But the pope's literary activities went beyond hagiography. They embraced studies liturgical (the Gregorian chant was the outcome) and exegetical; a treatise, profoundly influential, on the Book of Job; and the *Liber Regulae Pastoralis*, that wonderful exposition of the priest's calling—to a life not merely, as so often in the past, of doctrinal orthodoxy, but of moral integrity—which King Alfred later selected for translation into vernacular English. All this work set a precedent that medieval Rome could not forget. Future popes did not often live at the spiritual level of Gregory I. But few forgot that the defence of Christianity had a literary aspect which it was their duty to look to. However, the founding of the medieval papacy was of no interest to Gregory. For him, his literary labours, undertaken in passion, were no more than part of a mighty pastoral endeavour to save from damnation the souls of Romans and of barbarians. If they lack polish it is because their author had no time to lose. He was a sick man dying not, like his scattered flocks, from starvation but from physical infirmities, which he describes in his correspondence.

Historians like to draw attention to Gregory's incessant activity as landlord. His letters show us a pope who, for all his

apocalyptic vision, was daily ready to defend the patrimony of
his predecessors against Lombard marauders and to encourage
his agents to further efforts. The great territorial wealth of
the medieval papacy owes much to the man who was prepared
to defend his own—and more than his own, since the defence
of Rome itself was properly the business not of the pope but
of the Eastern Emperor. Herein, we are told, lay the seeds of
disintegration: mounting concern for territorial power was to
deprive the popes of their spiritual prestige. To Gregory, however, the problem did not present itself quite in this light.
At the very least, we may say that he viewed forcible dispossession much as any other Roman gentleman did, and had
the strength to defend the lands he had inherited. But there
was more to it than this. From the lands of the church and
from the alms of the faithful his flocks were, in a literal sense,
fed. Italy was a land whose people had long lived in a state of
chronic insecurity. Her roads were packed with vagabonds,
the dispossessed and the lost; and to them the churches alone
could afford help. Gregory faced this great social problem
morally, not economically. Belisarius had tried to transform
the famished unemployed of Rome into soldiers, fit to fight
under the imperial banners; but Gregory had no such utilitarian
aim. He organized, through churches and monasteries, a
system of poor-relief, hospitals and free distribution of bread
that cost them dear in treasure. It never flowed back into their
coffers. He repeatedly stated that his patrimony existed to help
the poor. For himself he claimed no prouder title than that of
dispensator in rebus pauperum, administrator of poor-relief.
This was his view of alms-giving: "The soil is common to all
men—when we give the necessities of life to the poor, we
restore to them what is already theirs—we should think of it
more as an act of justice than of compassion."

Against such a background, how did Gregory react to the
Lombards? Certainly not with unmitigated hostility. He probably thought of them much as St. Augustine thought of the
Vandals, as a terrible necessary scourge; and perhaps also as a
God-sent sign of the approaching end of the world, the victory
of Antichrist. "What is there left of delight in the world?"
he asks, in his sixth Homily on Ezekiel, "On all sides we see

war, on all sides we hear groans. Our cities are destroyed, the strong places razed, the countryside left desolate. There is none to till the fields; none, almost, to keep the towns. The survivors, poor dregs of humanity, are daily borne down. And yet the blows of divine justice have no end—Some are gone off into slavery, some left limbless, some killed. Again I ask, my brothers, what is there left of delight?—see to what straits Rome, once mistress of the world, is reduced. Worn down by her great and ceaseless sorrows, robbed of her sons, crushed by her enemies, ruined; and thus we see brought to pass the sentence long ago pronounced upon the city of Samaria by the prophet Ezekiel."

In the time that remained, Gregory laboured to save souls, wherever he could reach them. Hence his abiding interest in the Benedictine mission to the Anglo-Saxon settlers in Kent and in the beginning of the conversion of the Visigoths in Spain. These barbarians seemed very near to him. But nearer still were the untamed Lombards. "By what daily slaughter," he asks, in 602, "and by what ceaseless assaults have we not been oppressed by the Lombards in these five-and-thirty long years?" Comments of this kind are scattered throughout his writings. They were the wicked people, the people a man could not trust to keep an agreement, the destroyers of churches and of monasteries. Gregory had bargained with King Agilulf under the walls of Rome, and once, in 591, much though he hated bloodshed, was prepared to resist the Lombard duke of Spoleto with arms. Yet this is only half the story. If the Lombards were a scourge to the people of God they were also a field for missionary enterprise; and they, too, faced extermination. One of the most arresting passages in Paul's History is his account of the message Gregory sent to his representative in Constantinople, for transmission to the Emperor Maurice: "You may put this to his Highness, that if it had ever been my will to concern myself with killing, even with the death of Lombards, that people would today be split up in total confusion, and have no kings, no dukes, no counts". The pope then, according to Paul, thought even Lombards worth saving, not simply as individuals but as families and as a people. His work for their preservation lay largely in the stilling of the vendetta, the characteristic blood-feud that was the Germanic way of settling family differences and of preserving order. In limiting the effects of the vendetta, the Church unquestionably preserved the Germanic tribes from one form of suicide, but in so doing altered the nature and structure of their society.

At the time of their entering Italy, the Lombard chieftains were mostly Arian Christians and their followers either Arian or pagan. It can never satisfactorily be determined how far the Catholic hierarchy of Northern Italy survived, but it cannot have been to any appreciable extent. However, unavoidable diplomatic intercourse with Rome and with Byzantine Ravenna, and ordinary business dealings with Italians, must quickly have exposed the Lombards to Catholic influences; and by the time of Gregory the Great the possibility of their conversion, as a people, to Catholicism cannot have seemed too remote. As it happened, the pope was able to make use of a Bavarian (and Catholic) princess, Theudelinda, who became the queen of two successive Lombard rulers, Authari and Agilulf. (He similarly made use of the Frankish princess Bertha, great-grand-daughter of Clovis and wife of the Kentish Aethelberht.) It was not her religion that had caused the Lombards to seek Theudelinda for queen, but her blood, for through her mother, she was of the royal Lombard Lething dynasty. Furthermore, Bavarians and Lombards were old friends and neighbours, to whom the Alps proved no serious barrier. They made, together, a strong front against enemies like the Franks, and their social and economic ties were many. Gregory made what he could of the pious Theudelinda. At Monza, near Milan, she built a church, which she enriched with lands and treasure, including a series of silver ampullas of Syro-Palestinian workmanship sent to her by the pope. Sixteen of these survive. His gifts probably also included a book-cover or gospel-casket now known as Theudelinda's and a golden cross from Byzantium. Paul describes the barbaric paintings of scenes from Lombard history with which she caused her palace walls to be decorated.

But Theudelinda's religious leanings were not exclusively towards Rome. She lived in a part of Italy that had quarrelled with the papacy, where the metropolitans of Aquileia, Ravenna and Milan were unwilling to submit to Rome on certain important issues. And further, she was the friend of Irish monks. The Irishman Columbanus, fleeing from the Franks and always resolved to fight Arianism, was allowed to found a religious house at Bobbio, in Lombard territory. Some twenty years later Bobbio adopted the Benedictine Rule; but in origin it was strictly a foreign house, having no connection with Rome. The rôle of Bobbio in the history of culture, and especially of the transmission of manuscripts, is so momentous that we are apt to forget that it may have owed its original security to the desire of Agilulf and his wife to keep in touch, through Columbanus, with the life of Europe north of the Alps. A second monastery for which Theudelinda was responsible was San Dalmazzo at Pedona; and Paul says that there were others. But it was not till the time of King Perctarit (671–688) that the Lombards felt secure enough positively to encourage the foundation of religious houses and to welcome Roman missionaries. Certainly, Theudelinda's missionary endeavour was effective enough to cause a powerful anti-Catholic reaction among the Lombard chieftains; and it cannot be supposed that by the time of his death (ten years before Columbanus' arrival) Pope Gregory had made much progress. The only Christian hierarchy enjoying royal support was the Arian; and that hierarchy acknowledged not Rome but Pavia. The Lombards were not yet civilized.

A remarkable monument to the lasting spirit of Lombard separatism is the collection of customs made and written down in the reign of King Rothari (643), and known as Rothari's Edict. The oldest manuscript now extant (a St. Gall MS) was executed about fifty years later; but collation with other manuscripts reveals an original law-book of 388 chapters or titles, prefaced by an introductory chapter and a list of Lombard kings. This collection is extremely valuable, since it enables the historian not only to examine Lombard society at close quarters but also to compare it with other barbarian societies, notably the Scandinavian, Frankish and Anglo-Saxon, who chose, no doubt under comparable stimuli, to commit their customs to writing at about the same time. The total corpus of Western barbarian law has coherence for two reasons. First, because it rises, despite its tribalism, from a formal foundation of Roman Law, civil and canon; and secondly, because its various branches derive materially from a common and not very distant Germanic past.

Now, Rothari states in his preface and again in his epilogue, that the state of affairs in his kingdom, and especially the oppression of the poor by the rich, have caused him to correct the law as he knew it, to amend it and add to it and, when necessary, to subtract from it. (The barbarian legislators took this phrase from Justinian's 7th Novel.) The revised law he has had put together in one lawbook so that men, knowing it, might live together in peace. Having said this, the king gives a list of the preceding Lombard kings. There are sixteen of them, not all of the same family. The third is Leth, six of whose direct descendants wore his crown; but no special magic seems to be associated with the Lething name. Rothari himself was no Lething. He owed his crown not to blood but to election, that is to say, to his strong right arm and to his suitability in the eyes of his brother chieftains. However, although the first of his family to wear a crown, Rothari knew the names of his forebears to the eleventh generation, and believed that it would interest and impress his followers to have them in writing.

The Edict is written not in Lombardic but in Latin. The reason for this may be that Lombardic was not a literary language; Latin was the language of Western law. On the other hand, the Lombards were a proud people still. They did not love the Romans or the Greeks. The Kentish kings had managed to record their laws in their vernacular; and it is not, I think, absolutely certain that the Frankish kings had not done likewise. The true reason may be that the actual work of compilation was done by, and for the benefit of, clerks to whom that great exemplar, the Mosaic Law, was known only from the Latin Bible. Behind the barbarian laws lies the Book of Deuteronomy.

Rothari was an Arian, though his court was not proof against Catholic infiltration. In the invocatory *in dei nomine*, and in other ways, he acknowledges Christianity in his Edict; his thought moves on a moral level that is plainly the result of Christian influence. This is apparent in his elaborate measures to limit the effect of the family vendetta. He provides a tariff of money compensations that shall satisfy the honour of a free family, a member of which has incurred physical injury however slight, and he closes his tariff with the words: "for all the above-noted wounds, of cut or thrust, as they may come between free men, we have provided a higher composition than did our forebears, so that when such composition has been received the *faida* (that is, enmity) shall be abandoned, and no more shall be demanded and no ill-feeling be harboured; and that the quarrel shall be considered at an end and friendship shall be established." There is no suggestion here that the taking of vengeance is wrong in itself but simply that it would be wrong to pursue it after the parties to a quarrel had agreed to accept an alternative form of satisfaction. Chapter 189 of the Edict expressly allows the family of a free woman to take vengeance if she sleeps with a man not her husband; and a husband was permitted to kill an unfaithful wife. Nearly two centuries later, Paul told with approval the tale of a little dwarf who, to avenge his master Godepert, hid in the canopy over a font in order to leap down and stab his master's foe, and, having so done, fell to the swords of his victim's retainers, "but although he died, he still signally avenged the wrong done to his master". The vendetta died a slow death in Italy as elsewhere, and only over the course of centuries did it come to seem both immoral and unnecessary. To Rothari and his contemporaries it was merely wasteful of life and property, and dangerous to a small society isolated in a hostile world.

The vendetta is only one of the many matters treated in the Edict, though for us it is among the most instructive. Rothari deals also with offences against his peace, with manslaughter, obstruction, bodily injuries to the unfree; and, moving to the law of inheritance, with the equal dividing of property between all male heirs, with the necessity of making donations in the presence of many witnesses; and finally with the law relating to the position of women, and to the nature of manumission.

All this points to a society far advanced from the tribal state, and already receptive to the influences and experience of Rome. Yet the appearance is somewhat deceptive. The savage is beneath the surface. Take, for example, chapter 381 of the

Edict: "If a man call another man *arga* (coward) in anger and cannot deny it but admits that he said it in anger, he shall swear and say that he is in fact no coward; and further shall pay twelve *solidi* in compensation for that word. But if he persists in its use he shall justify it, if he can, in a duel, or he shall undoubtedly pay compensation." Only with so large a sum could the king hope to stave off the endless vendetta that would normally follow the utterance of an angry word. Again, chapter 376 reads: "Let no man presume to kill another man's slave-woman or servant on the ground that she is a witch (or *masca* as we say); for Christian minds refuse to believe it possible that a woman could eat a living man from inside him". Christian minds might indeed decline to believe in vampires; but not Lombard minds.

Rothari's Edict appeared in the same year as a Life of St. Columbanus by Jonas of Bobbio. The two constitute a modest renaissance for Lombard Italy. The Edict, for all its barbarism, is law-giving such as the Romans would have understood; while the Life, written in a monastery, is no very polished performance. Both are evidence of more settled times and are a kind of admission that the barbarians knew that they had come to their journey's end: from Italy there was no advance and no retreat; and terms were being arrived at with Roman civilization in all its aspects, legal, ecclesiastical, artistic, commercial.

It is impossible here to examine the further development of Lombard law. Rothari, as has been seen, contributed the first 388 chapters to the corpus. He was followed, in the course of a century by Grimoald (9 chapters), Liutprand (153), Ratchis (14) and Aistulf (22); and to this list should be added a small body of laws emanating from the Lombard duchy of Benevento. All are the work of barbarians, and of barbarians less advanced than the Franks or Burgundians; yet they show, more clearly than any narrative, the yielding of first one and then another fundamental social principle to the inexorable pressure of Western civilization. Brought up to the cult of the sword, basing their moral life upon the simplest principles, of blood, valour and fidelity, the Lombards put not too much value upon human life. Yet, as the years passed (their official conversion to Catholicism may be placed in 653) the life of the individual seemed to them to matter more and to require increasingly the protection of what we should call, and what the Romans called, the state. As a corollary, the life of the family, as the smallest social and legal unit, seemed to matter less.

Repeated royal efforts to limit the vendetta weakened not only the family but also the *fara*, the group of families. A still graver blow was administered by the Church, when it encouraged the making of donations, by individuals, both of family property and of sons to become monks. As monastic foundations increased in social importance, so the barbarian family diminished. ("Personal profession or the devotion of the father makes the monk", commented Gratian.) Yet another blow came when the Church limited the ways by which the family perpetuated its stock, by forbidding polygamy, concubinage and repudiation.

Two barbarian social concepts that the Church could not easily affect were the *mundium* and the *guidrigild* (equivalent to the Anglo-Saxon *wergild*). The *mundium* was the dominion or protection exercised by the family, the husband or the king over women, and thus the value or price of women, or of any person not *sui iuris* (e.g. a slave), in civil law. A free woman could no more be without her *mundium* than she could be without her soul. When she married her husband acquired it, at a price, from her family. The *mundium* was certainly a woman's or a slave's effective defence; but it was also an affirmation of the superior right of the family, or in its absence, of the king, over the individual. It could be a very hard right, and the instinct of the Church was against it.

The *guidrigild* was the individual's blood-value or price in criminal law; and it would vary according to social position. It rested on the concept that the spilling of blood and even killing could be compensated for without involving the guilty in blame or punishment. The Church welcomed the substitution of compensation based on the *guidrigild* for the vendetta, but at the same time insisted that a moral issue was involved in the spilling of blood; punishment must follow. Hence the compilation of the penitential books (early among them, that of St. Columbanus), which provided for God's punishment, according to a fixed tariff and irrespective of the view of the crime taken by family or state. God must have satisfaction.

This had been the view of St. Augustine, and to it the doctors and legists of the Church adhered. This, as much as anything, in time induced the Lombards to look upon the spilling of blood and the taking of life from what may be termed the Western point of view.

Apart from the vendetta, the Church disliked no method of determining right so much as the duel, or trial by battle. But it, too, was deeply ingrained in all the Western barbarians. Liutprand puts the issue thus: if a man is accused of murder, the penalty for which is the loss of all his property, and challenged to a duel and is defeated, he shall not forfeit all his property but only the *guidrigild* of the victim, as under the old law, "for we cannot be certain about the Judgement of God and we have heard of a man losing his suit by combat unjustly. Yet we cannot forbid the custom of combat, because it is an old custom of our Lombard race". The Church could not destroy the duel, but it did humanize it.

The Judgement of God, or ordeal, to which Liutprand refers, was a related procedure for determining right where all else had failed and the vendetta seemed imminent. The Church did not invent it but adapted it and controlled its application, irrational as it obviously was. Whether by water or fire, the Christian ordeal was a solemn religious ceremony, for it put the onus of proof of innocence or guilt on God; and it was unquestionably less bloodthirsty than the duel.

Another practice over which the Church had to arrive at a compromise was slavery. Slaves were the most valuable article of commerce known to the barbarians, and warfare was conducive to a plentiful supply of them. Pope Gregory was not surprised to see the Lombards leading away their captives to slavery, like dogs on leashes, after an expedition to Rome. But Catholic Lombardy was a slightly more peaceful place than Gregory had known, and slaves were becoming more expensive and less easy to obtain. It should not be thought that their lot was ever happy; we may recall the words of the Digest— *servitutem mortalitati fere comparamus*—'We may say that in effect slavery is death'. But their help was needed to keep land in cultivation, and the servile or semi-servile farmer working and living upon his tenement was not uncommon and not invariably badly off. In theory there was no defence for slavery —that is, for regarding a man and his children as the chattels of another, with no standing at law. But in practice slavery was ineradicable, save over centuries. The Church, therefore, did what could be done to ameliorate the slave's lot, especially in the marriage-market. Manumission was encouraged as a means to salvation for the slave-owner. Many charters of manumission have survived. But manumission varied greatly in form. It was seldom complete. That is to say, the freedman, though enjoying a new status at law, might well wish to remain working his lord's land. A bond of obedience (*obsequium*) remained; the proprietor could still call on his freedman, his *aldio*, for service in his war-host or in his court, and might even put his rent up. The freedman, for his part, still enjoyed his lord's protection. So the bargain was not a bad one. In one Lombard charter of manumission, the newly-enfranchised declare: "Vulpo, Mitildis, their sons and daughters and kindred, stated that they did not wish to follow the four roads to complete freedom, but in future would be content to have their freedom under the care and protection of the priests and deacons of the Church of Great St. Mary at Cremona".

Manumission of course cost money. The manumission charters are one of several kinds of evidence pointing to an apparently free and plentiful movement of gold in Lombard territory, such as one would expect in lands adjoining the Byzantine Exarchate. However, it is easy to be misled. Though the Lombards learned to calculate values in gold, the substance was always precious to them as treasure. It was still the longed-for booty in war, the expected gift of the foreigner anxious to impress. Gold supplies were, further, being drained out of Western Europe into Byzantium where they remained, mostly immobilized as church treasure, till partially released by the Islamic invaders. We know that the *solidus* of Lombard Italy contained (what would have horrified the minters of classical Rome) only four grammes of gold. But this does not tell us about its purchasing power. What would a *solidus* buy? In 718, an olive orchard was sold for 8 *solidi*; in 749, two horses fetched 50 *solidi*, though a horse with trappings might fetch 100 *solidi*; half a house cost 9 *solidi* in 720, and a vegetable

garden in 725, 15 *solidi*. The highest composition was 1200
solidi for killing one's wife—an almost impossible sum, except
for a very rich man. Others were 900 *solidi* for breaking open a
burial vault, and the same sum for an outrage committed
upon a free woman. Rothari ordered a fine of 1 *solidus* for causing the miscarriage of a mare, and 3 *solidi* for the same offence
against a female slave. One is left with the impression that the
economic life of Lombard Italy, centred upon its mills, pastures,
horses, orchards and slaves, was not critically affected by the
circulation of gold. Not many Lombard coins survive, those
that do being *tremissi* (a *tremissis* was one-third of a *solidus*),
mostly of gold but a few of silver. In workmanship they are
much inferior to the worst that the Byzantines could do. The
Lombards, in brief, knew about money and loved gold, but
lived still to some extent by barter.

The Lombards' relentless enemies, the people they most
feared, were the Byzantines. It was not military skill or overwhelming force that had given Italy to the Lombards, but the
exhaustion of imperial arms, plague and famine. "The Romans
had then no courage to resist, because the pestilence which had
occurred at the time of Narses had destroyed very many",
writes Paul. And so the Romans (that is, the inhabitants of
Italy) made terms. But Byzantium regarded this as no more
than a temporary setback, and laid deep plans for a second
reconquest. She had her cities to fall back upon, wealth with
which to bring other barbarians into the field against the
Lombards, and command of the sea. Italy was already organized
for local defence in a network of *castra* manned by imperial
and local troops; and to these the terrified countrymen could
retreat. Only famine could, and did, bring about their capitulation. Thus fell the great walled city of Pavia, where Alboin
established the seat of the Lombard kings,[1] and other cities,
like Spoleto in the centre and Benevento in the south, where
Lombard chieftains or dukes succeeded to the position of their
Byzantine predecessors.

[1]There is no doubt that the Lombards had an advantage enjoyed by
no other barbarians in their capital of Pavia, where Roman traditions continued. The Law School, for example, was able to furnish trained notaries
for the royal writing office.

It is unlikely that the Lombards (even Liutprand) had a clear objective, such as the conquest of all Italy, before their eyes. They were, to begin with, divided amongst themselves; and for a time they even managed without kings, until fear of extinction gave them a sense of the need for military and political coherence.

The four cities that offered the stiffest resistance to the Lombards, and where Roman traditions were never allowed to die, were Rome, Naples, Genoa and Ravenna. The defence of Rome was undertaken by the popes, that of Genoa and Naples by the inhabitants, while Ravenna, safe behind marshes, became the headquarters of the Exarch, the military and civil representatives of the Emperor in Italy.

For two centuries the Emperors, heavily committed in the East, spared what time and money they could for the reconquest of Italy. Sometimes they came near to success. It was possible to bribe the Franks to enter Italy from the North-west and ravage the Po valley. Once, in 663, the Emperor Constans II entered Rome at the head of an army, but after twelve days thought it prudent to retire to Sicily. The Lombards occasionally, as under Percatarit, made peace with Ravenna. But in truth stalemate was inevitable. The Emperors could never quite manage to make good their claims in Italy, and the Lombards could never throw off their fear of what would happen if the Emperors did manage to do so. Between the two stood the papacy, at first the loyal lieutenant of the Empire but soon, and increasingly, the independent upholder of *Romanitas* in the West. Theological differences emphasized the growing gap between Rome and Byzantium, though it is very doubtful whether Rome ever completely abandoned hope of a second reconquest. Byzantine help would probably always have been preferred to the dreadful alternative of calling in the Franks.

In one respect Byzantium may be said to have had her victory. She civilized her enemies. The art of the Lombards as it developed over the seventh and eighth centuries, bore increasing evidence of the proximity of Ravenna, city of imperial craftsmen. In Lombard grave-goods, for example, interlace was replaced by Byzantine plant or animal ornamentation. Nor was the victory confined to Lombard Italy.

Sicily and Calabria remained in culture Greek. Thousands of Greek monks, fleeing from the iconoclast persecution, settled in Southern Italy and penetrated as far north as Rome. It is not going too far to say that Rome was hellenized afresh between 600 and 750. Partly, this was the work of the Exarchs, whose links with Rome were closer than is sometimes thought. But still more was it due to the popes themselves. During the period, no less than thirteen of them were Greek-speaking easterners. The Rule of St. Basil displaced that of St. Benedict in many a Roman monastery; and Pope Zacharius (741–751) translated into Greek Pope Gregory's Life of St. Benedict.

It is no longer possible, as it once was, to dismiss Lombard civilization as entirely derivative. Nor can it be said to have left no trace. Lombard place-names are widely scattered throughout Italy; they can even be found in areas never politically subject to the Lombards; and there are plenty of Lombard words in the Italian language. All the same, the Lombards made no impression comparable with that of the Franks on Northern Gaul. They were fewer in number and more formidably opposed; also, they were more primitive. Yet how shall we be certain, as we look at the various layers of Germanic influence upon Italy, that we can truthfully distinguish Goth from Lombard, and Lombard from Frank? Archaeologists find that their doubts increase rather than diminish. The historian, too, would be wise to defer judgement.

Paul the Deacon, writing his history in a Monte Cassino which his people had both destroyed and restored, seemed to feel no shame in the eclipse of the native dynasty. Charlemagne, after all, was as much a German as was Liutprand, and he ruled his new subjects as a *Rex Langobardorum* without thought or hope of their becoming Franks. Perhaps it was as well that the Lombards should have succumbed to barbarians like themselves and not to Byzantium. The Lombard lords remained where they were, farming their properties, doing business with the cities and ports of the peninsula, hearing in the evenings the epic songs of their past, of which almost no trace remains. Still half-civilized—none of their kings was more fearsome than Aistulf, who died as late as 756—they had done, in a short time, nearly as much as the popes themselves for

Roman Christianity in northern Italy. The great Benedictine houses that sprang up in eighth-century Italy were of Lombard or of Frankish foundation. Hungry as they always were (and had to be) for land, the chieftains found enough to spare from their patrimonies to endow the miracle-working shrines of the countryside and to make them the homes of scribes through whom much of what Europe has of ancient learning was to be preserved. And these were the descendants of the tribe once branded by Velleius Paterculus as *gens etiam germana feritate ferocior*, the people fiercer even than German savagery.

CHAPTER IV

THE FRANKS (1)

THE Franks were by no means the first to disturb the peace of the seventeen provinces of Roman Gaul. The remoteness of her northern parts from Rome and the geographical peculiarities of her land-frontiers (her great amphitheatre of mountains does not at all points form a natural barrier) ensured that Gaul would fall a prey to invasion from the North or East, and that, when she did, her excellent road-system would prove more of a hindrance than a help. Throughout the period of the Later Empire she combined an uneasy spirit of independence with a singular inability to manage her own affairs. Her western provinces, for example, were in a state of chronic disturbance, and it is not unlikely that the restlessness of the *Bagaudae* (robber bands and a slave population in revolt), had much to do with the failure of the last Gallo-Roman governors to withstand external pressure. Quite apart, however, from political isolation and social chaos, Gaul also lacked racial cohesion; the distinctness, in interest and nature, of her component races (Celtic-Gaulish, with an already strong admixture of Germanic *coloni* in the countryside and Graeco-Syrians in the towns) was not much diminished by the victory of Latin over her other languages. That there was still a Roman, or romanized, administration in Gaul in the fourth and fifth centuries is certain, just as it is also certain that trade still flourished in her cities and that the Gallo-Roman aristocracy continued to live in comfort, to cultivate the arts of Rome in their villas, and to provide the greater part of the personnel for the administration of the *civitates* and the bishoprics. Gaul was still rich and still belonged to *Romania*, the Mediterranean world. But she was incapable of helping herself.

Reference has already been made to the passage through Gaul of the East Germans—Vandals, who continued through Spain to Africa, and Goths, who were allowed to settle in southern Gaul before finally moving on into Spain. Our concern is now mainly with the West Germans, the settlers along the banks of the Rhine and in the sandy wastes to the North of the Rhine estuary. Roman writers, adepts at giving names to peoples and things, were never quite certain who these West Germans were, or how to classify them. One group of tribes they called the *Franci*, a name perhaps derived from the Germanic *frak* or *frech*, meaning 'savage' or 'proud', but whether these *Franci*, or Franks, ever had more than an occasional sense of unity (and then military) is very doubtful. Living nearest the North Sea, along the course of the river Ijssel, were the Salian (or salty) Franks; or that, at least, is what Ammianus says the Emperor Julian called them. Several Emperors found it a hard struggle to keep them to the North of the Rhine; and finally, during the troubles of the late third century, large numbers of them succeeded in crossing and settling in the uninviting plain of northern Texandria. Pressure from behind and the easy river-courses (e.g. the Scheldt and Lys) leading south to richer agricultural land, soon caused the first Salians, perhaps some 100,000 in number, to leave Texandria behind them and to seek their fortunes, as Roman *federati*, in what is now Belgium. And so they continued without much check, until they came to a region flanked by hills and forest (the *Silva Carbonaria*) and covered by the great Roman road running approximately west-east, from Boulogne to Cologne, through Bavay and Tongres. Here they met with opposition and were forced to halt, establishing themselves under their chieftains in strongholds such as Tournai. Both place-names and the present division of languages in Belgium bear witness to that halt, though the absence of any systematic examination of barbarian cemeteries in this area forbids assessment of their original numbers. They had reached the northern parts of the province of *Belgica Secunda*, which contained important cities, like Reims and Soissons, and was well populated. Further advance, therefore, could only take the form of raiding or of occasional settlement among communities which were not easily to be displaced. Indeed the further south the Salians moved the less chance did they have of surviving absorption into an already mixed, but Latin-speaking, stock. It may be said, in brief, that Salian settlements, usually small and isolated, were common as far south as the Seine, not infrequent in the disturbed area between the Seine and the Loire, and exceedingly infrequent south of the Loire.[1] They are identifiable by place-name study (the -*court* or -*ville* suffix to a Frankish proper name is only one of many examples) and by the study of grave-goods in Frankish cemeteries.

The Frank was accustomed to be buried in a manner that at once distinguished his remains from those of a Gallo-Roman, and also, though much less certainly, from those of other Germans. He was laid, as a rule, facing east, wrapped in his cloak (the metal buckle of which alone survives) and placed, usually, uncoffined in the earth. Provisions for his future life would be placed about him in pots, and he would also have his weapons, in the making of which his people showed great skill. These would be a short sword (the *scramasax*), a throwing-hatchet (the *francisca*, the characteristic Frankish weapon) and very occasionally a longsword; but this last was the weapon of the horsemen, and the Franks of the period were, with few exceptions, accustomed to move and fight on foot. They offer a marked contrast, in this respect, with the Alamanni, and still more with the non-Germanic Huns, who lived on horseback. Finally, the Frankish cemetery may afford other unmistakable evidence of barbarian heathenism: ceremonial decapitation after death, and ritual fires. Thus the Frank, still unassimilated or only partially assimilated into the Gallo-Roman stock, betrays himself to the archaeologist, to the student of place-names and, though much less confidently, to the anthropologist. But he lives for us equally in the pages of his national historian, Gregory of Tours; and to him we must turn before we trace the course of the great advance from Tournai to Reims and beyond.

Gregory lived in the second half of the sixth century, which means that his Frankish contemporaries belonged to the third generation to live in Gaul. He was himself a Gallo-Roman aristocrat from the Auvergne, where his family had long held

---

[1]One scholar, who believes on linguistic grounds in a mass-migration of Franks, holds that they may have comprised as much as twenty-five per cent of the population of Gaul.

high office, lay and ecclesiastical. He succeeded, in due course,
to what might almost be called a family seat, the Bishopric of
Tours, in western Gaul. With his work as a bishop (which he
would have placed first in importance) and as a politician we
cannot be concerned here. What must interest us is that he
was also a writer. There survive from his pen several works of
hagiography—notably a new Life of St. Martin of Tours, his
own patron—some writings of a more specialized nature, and a
History of the Franks (the title is not his).

This History is one of the great narratives of the Dark Ages
and recalls, both in inspiration and treatment, the other histories
of the western barbarian settlers—those notably, of the Goths,
the Lombards and the English. Gregory did not, of course,
set about writing an impartial account of Frankish affairs: he
is no more 'modern' than is Bede, like whom he is sometimes
credited with thoughts that could never have entered his
superstitious head. He makes, in short, some severe demands on
the intelligence of the historian. But this much, at least, may
be said with confidence of his approach to the task he set
himself: he was, before all else, a Catholic Christian living in a
Gaul still far from secure from the (to him) horrible heresy of
the Arians; and he viewed the Franks (already fused with his
own people, apart from the greatest families of both races)
not as the destroyers but, perhaps despite themselves, as the
saviours of Christian Gaul. For they had become directly
converted to Catholicism without passing through any Arian
stage, and under their first great chieftain had championed the
Catholic cause while at the same time pursuing their own more
mundane interests. They had passed over the decadent Gallo-
Romans like a purging fire; had accepted the guidance of the
Catholic hierarchy; and Gregory was grateful. What he could
neither understand nor stomach (any more than can some more
recent historians) was the apparent lapse of the Frankish
chieftains of the second and third generations into a state of
chronic civil war that plainly did not serve the interests of the
Church and could thus only be condemned as immoral. Like
Gildas in Britain, Gregory was concerned to call back his
contemporaries from the evil of their ways; and this he did
by displaying before them their own comparatively recent

history—not the disconnected epic of their bards, but a purposeful tale of advance to Christianity. They were men of blood indeed, but men with a mission. This constant harping upon the glories of their grandparents' days is what makes Gregory's approach to his own contemporaries so misleading, and gives his stories so compelling an atmosphere of social transition.

With this much as background, we may return to the history of the Frankish advance, always bearing in mind that it is substantially Gregory's narrative with only occasional corroboration from other sources.

Tournai fell to the Franks in the year 446. The chieftains who took it and made it their headquarters managed to establish a dynasty, the first years of which are naturally lost in myth. An early member of the house was Meroveus ('the sea-fighter'), who led his people to fight side by side with the Gallo-Romans as loyal *federati* against Attila and the Huns on the Mauriac Plain, near Troyes. He left his name to his descendants, the Merovingians (the author of *Beowulf* knew them as such). His son, Childeric, proved more troublesome to the Romans and had to be ejected forcibly from northern Gaul, leaving behind many Frankish settlers. That he was no mere savage is amply demonstrated by the magnificence of his burial chamber, discovered in Tournai in 1653. It contained ornaments, weapons and a hoard of coins that witness to wide contacts with the Empire as well as with the barbarian world. Childeric was a rich man.

With his son, Clovis—or more properly, Chlodovech, 'noble warrior'—we reach Gregory's hero, a barbarian chieftain of heroic stature.

The question may well be asked, "Why use the title *chieftain* rather than *king*?" Successful leadership in war, ruthlessly pursued, was undoubtedly the first quality expected of any barbarian leader, though it was not the only one; and this would entitle him, if not his children, to whatever formal show of personal supremacy his people were accustomed to allow. Whether this would or would not justify us in calling him a king rather than a chieftain (what the Romans called a *regulus*) is a matter of opinion. A sacral element has been inferred, from pre-Christian Swedish king-making ceremonies, to have played some part at least in the rites of other Germanic peoples, who had not forgotten the land from which they once set out. But the comparative study of kingship in Germanic lands has still a long way to go before it can be determined how wide-spread the magic element in such ceremonies was, and whether it reveals an outlook on leadership that would place, for example, the Frankish chieftains on a higher, more mystical footing than is at present suggested by the ease with which, when unsuccessful, they were disposed of. The Germanic peoples had, of course, a word from which our word 'king' is descended; but its original meaning is so obscure that it seems best not to employ it and thus risk endowing it with any part of its later meaning.

Clovis succeeded his father in 482, at the age of fifteen, not as *Rex Francorum*, for there was no such person, but as leader of the Frankish tribes acknowledging the supremacy of Tournai. (It may be noted that some near neighbours held aloof from him, and later suffered for it.) Within five years he had led a force south into the Soissonnais to defeat Syagrius, the last independent Roman ruler in Gaul. The Frank was after booty, of course, and more lands with which to reward his retainers. He got what he wanted and, in addition, soon found himself the acknowledged successor of Syagrius in northern Gaul. Certain of the Gallo-Roman bishops, notably St. Rémi of Reims, were probably responsible for bringing about the recognition of a *fait accompli*; in one sense no very difficult feat, since Clovis had naturally taken over from Syagrius the lands of the imperial *fiscus*, but, in another, very difficult—for Clovis was a pagan, unacknowledged by the Emperor in Byzantium.

Our appreciation of Clovis' subsequent career must turn largely on when, and why, we think that he became converted to Christianity; and this is no easy matter, since the chronology of his reign is hard to establish. Gregory probably placed the conversion ten years too early, and was thus able to envisage all succeeding campaigns as crusades. Modern scholarship, on the other hand, has made a strong case for moving the date of the conversion forward to about 503—that is, to within about eight years of his death. It does not follow that Gregory falsified

history, but rather that his mind, obsessed with the consequences of that conversion, refused to admit the possibility
that Clovis could have undertaken any major campaign in
Gaul unless it were for the furtherance of Catholicism. Gregory
thus recognized the fierce savagery of his hero's conquests
but interpreted it as divine vengeance; and found in him a
saving virility, most desirable of barbarian qualities, that made
him all the fitter to lead Gaul against the Arian oppressors,
the Visigoths. For our part, we can accept Gregory's view that
Clovis was a great and magnificent fighter (*magnus et pugnator
egregius* are his own words), the kind of warrior of whom tradition and legend would make much, perhaps even before his
death. But we should do well to look for other motives than that
which naturally appealed to Gregory. When conversion finally
came to him, it is likely enough that Clovis devoutly accepted
the Christian God as the giver of victory (most precious of
gifts) and as a better god than any his fathers had known,
under whose providence and with whose priests it was proper
to fight on. Yet this in no way diminished the driving-force
that had brought him from Tournai: desire for booty and the
good things of civilization, and hatred of other barbarian
peoples, derived perhaps from feuds of great antiquity.

Clovis was not long content with the lands he had taken
from Syagrius. He spent years—how many it is impossible to
say—in subduing the troublesome inhabitants of western
Gaul as far south as the Loire, where he would have come
into direct contact with the Visigoths of Aquitaine. This is the
obscurest part of his career. But his main concern was with
the barbarians of eastern Gaul and the Rhineland.

One branch of the Franks, known as the Ripuarians, had
not followed the Salians into Texandria and thus south into
Belgica Secunda. Instead, they had approached the Middle
Rhine from the east in the general area of Cologne, and finally
crossed it, establishing themselves among the cities and villas
on the west bank. The ruin of Roman trade and culture in the
Rhineland, and the destruction of city life there, are no longer
thought to have been quite as catastrophic as they once were.
The towns suffered much, buildings were destroyed, walls fell
into disrepair and the population was considerably reduced.

Yet life went on in Cologne, Trier, Metz and other cities. We know, for example, that the Syrian glass-makers of Cologne survived and found ready markets in the Moselle valley and further afield. The Franks would not, perhaps, have had much liking for sub-Roman town-life or for life among the half-deserted villas, such as the great villa of Nennig in Luxembourg. But it was better than life in the forest-clearings of central Germany.

The *Silva Carbonaria* formed for a time a natural barrier between Salians and Ripuarians, though it may not have proved very effective. Somewhere in Lorraine the two branches of the Franks met and fused; and probably not long afterwards the Ripuarians decided to place themselves under the protection of Clovis, which it took him many years to enforce. The enemies they feared were the Alamanni, the fiercest of the West German tribes. (*All-mann* meant 'Men from everywhere', 'men united', and presumably referred to the many offshoots of the Swabian branch of the West Germans from which they were constituted.) The Alamanni were well-armed (e.g. their big cemetery at Schretzheim) and they were also horsemen. And thus, when they started to move from Alsace in a north-westerly direction the Ripuarians were alarmed; but together with the Salians faced them. The result was the famous battle of Tolbiac (modern Zülpich), at which the Franks defeated the Alamanni and advanced their power as far south as Bâle. Gregory believed that Clovis owed this victory to a sudden decision to call for help upon Christ, and that his baptism at Reims followed not long afterwards. This may have been so. But, even if it was not, the destruction of at least the northern part of the Alamannic confederation and the immediate surrender of the southern part, panic-stricken, to the overlordship of Theodoric, removed an important barrier that had hitherto stood between the Franks and the Ostrogoths. Theodoric, alarmed, is known to have warned Clovis to proceed no further; and Clovis, boldly deciding to challenge the whole Gothic empire, took the logical step of throwing in his lot with the enemies of Gothic Arianism —namely, the Catholic hierarchy of Gaul and, more remotely, the Emperor himself in Constantinople. In this way the Franks entered upon the scene of Mediterranean politics.

At about the same time, Clovis also attacked the Burgundians, a once-powerful East German people that had come to settle in the Rhône valley, where they had become heavily romanized. The Burgundians are a people of great interest to the archaeologist and linguist as well as to the historian; but here it can only be noted that in pursuing a family feud in which his queen, a Burgundian, was involved, Clovis risked removing yet one more barrier between the Franks and the Goths.

The final struggle came, as it happened, with the Visigoths. Tradition asserted (as it often did in these cases) that Clovis slew the Visigothic King, Alaric II, with his own hand on the field of Vouillé, near Poitiers. The victory was striking enough in any event. The Visigothic power in Aquitaine, though not, of course, in Spain, was broken, and Clovis was able to pillage his victim's treasury at Toulouse before returning in triumph to give thanks at the shrine of St. Martin at Tours. Aquitaine did not become francified; nor did she suffer more than spasmodic supervision at the hands of her new overlords. But she was henceforth ranged with Catholic against Arian Europe.

Aquitaine is not all the Midi. Some of the greatest cities of southern France lie in Provence, most Roman of Rome's provinces. And Theodoric, with the Burgundians, took good care that Provence, at least, should not fall to the Franks. Geographically it was so much a part of Italy that Clovis decided to risk nothing further and not to seek a country that the Ostrogoths could so easily defend. Thus the Mediterranean coast-line and its rich ports stretching from Genoa to Barcelona remained in Gothic hands. Clovis never reached the Mediterranean.

While he was at Tours, Clovis received the legate of the Emperor Anastasius, who had brought with him letters bestowing on Clovis the title of consul; "and from that day", says Gregory, "he was hailed as consul or Augustus". Historians have been much exercised in the interpretation of this passage. Whatever its *nuances*, the general sense is that the Emperor was recognizing one more barbarian chieftain as the effective ruler of a Roman province. It implies, further, that the Emperor had for some time been in touch with the Franks and was glad

to recognize them, at the appropriate moment, as a counter-
balance to Gothic power in the West. The Franks had come to
stay, and the Gallo-Romans, ever loyal to the idea of Empire,
would be well-advised to admit as much and to co-operate
with them. One further interest in the matter was that of the
Church of Tours. It is not inconceivable that the guardians of
St. Martin, Gaul's premier saint, had played some part in the
preceding negotiations and had long visualized Clovis as a
Frankish Constantine. If so, they succeeded only in part. One
would like to know whether the ambition was cherished at
Tours up to the time of Charlemagne and Alcuin, when it
might indeed be said to have been realized. Gregory himself
constituted a link in that literary tradition.

Clovis did not stay at Tours but hurried north into Neustria,
the newly-won Frankish settlement-area to which Paris was
the key. There, on the hill of Ste. Geneviève, he built a church.
In due course it came to hold his bones. He was forty-five when
he died—for a barbarian, a mature age. No reader of Gregory
of Tours could pretend that Christianity had softened his heart
or deflected him from his natural aspirations. He lived and
died a Frankish chieftain, a warrior of the Heroic Age, a man
of blood and a seeker after gold. But he had made Francia,
and made it within the Roman Empire.

One consequence of this personal achievement was that the
newly-won lands were divided, at his death, between his four
sons. The sub-Roman administration of Gaul, in so far as it
had survived, operated at the *civitas* level and was therefore
not disturbed by the dismemberment. Probably the Gallo-
Romans would have agreed with the Franks that in practice
it was not dismemberment at all, and entailed no declension.
Administrative disunity was not in itself either new or distress-
ing; but civil war, its social consequence, was quite another
matter—at least to the Gallo-Romans. We have, then, to face a
special difficulty in considering Gaul in the century following
the death of Clovis: it is, that she had become the homeland of
barbarians with a complicated heritage of family-feuds which
were accentuated by fresh problems of land-tenure. The
fratricidal quarrels of the century were not quite as aimless or
immoral as Gregory made out. They were the business of

barbarian life, even to barbarians who were speedily becoming romanized.

Some idea of this life is given in the collection of Frankish customs known as the *Lex Salica*, or Salian Law. It should be emphasized that the collection, as it has come down to us, is by no means certainly the unamended work of the sixth century. In general it may truthfully reflect the usages of the sixth century, but it was worked over and added to throughout that and succeeding centuries. The bombastic prologue of the longer version probably belongs to the eighth century, and the format of the whole collection possibly to the ninth. Even so, it is not an officially promulgated code, in the sense in which the Theodosian Code is, but a collection of customs designed rather for consultation and study by the clergy. In this respect the Salian Law code is like most of the other barbarian codes, which belong approximately to the same period; they are related in matter and inspiration, and are most profitably studied as a single manifestation of interest in customary law.

Frankish daily life, as it emerges from the Salian Law, is much like that of the contemporary Anglo-Saxons or Burgundians, and not far removed from that of the Lombards. It rested on a juridical distinction between Frank and Roman which must already have become blurred, and which did not, in fact, retard the fusion of the two races. The Frankish tariff of injuries and the appropriate compensations is even more elaborate than the Lombardic; so, equally, is its tariff of thefts, the compensation for which varies according to the condition and age of the property stolen. The severest penalty is exacted only for theft of grave-goods. The family is the social unit which most requires protection, even at the cost of the individual. If the individual wishes to abandon his family he can do so, but only in the most solemn and formal manner, before witnesses. The patrimony is protected from alienation through marriage by the most famous of the Salian rules (number 92)— namely, that no woman could inherit land while there lived a possible male heir. The patrimony, like that of Clovis himself, could be divided among sons without leaving the control of the family. Village families could combine to keep out a stranger who wished to settle among them, a single adverse vote being sufficient to send him on his way. Yet it must not be thought that the Franks aimed at deliberate segregation from the Gallo-Romans. Their customs were enforced and interpreted at regular meetings of mixed tribunals of Franks and Romans. It was for such bodies of *boni homines*, or *rachinburgii* as the Franks called them, to declare the law as they found it; and this must have called for constant compromise and adaptation in a society of mixed races, mixed languages[1] and, above all, of mixed marriages. The process of integration could not be stopped at the juridical level, even if it had been desired. We must not suppose that *Lex Salica* is, or represents, the unalterable code by which all Franks lived all the time. It simply gives us a valuable general idea of how they lived at one particular time.

The sons of Clovis ruled independently over their shares of partitioned Gaul from the cities of Metz, Orleans, Paris and Soissons. But they had also inherited from their father a religion and a view of the non-Frankish world that caused them from time to time to act as one. They agreed to give their sister in marriage to Amalaric, the Visigoth king of Spain, and sent her off with 'a heap of fine ornaments', as befitted a barbarian princess. Soon, however, they found it necessary to rescue her from the Arians, and brought her back with even more ornaments. They agreed also upon an expedition against the Burgundians, which resulted in the political extinction of that once powerful people, and in the extension of Frankish power over Provence, and notably over a great Mediterranean port, Marseilles. We may explain such unprovoked aggression in a number of ways; by fear, by tribal hatred, by vendetta, or by the always urgent need for plunder to reward followers, and for slaves. Each year in the springtime the Franks set out in their war-bands upon some such venture; for fighting was as much the business of good, as carousing was of foul weather.[2]

The chieftain who ruled in Metz over the Eastern, or Austrasian, Frankish settlements faced greater dangers than

[1]Frankish was still understood in northern Gaul in the ninth century.
[2]*The Campus Martius*, their spring assembly, is often wrongly translated as the *Marchfield*; but in fact it was the *Field of Mars*, the *Warfield*, and was not less so when, as later happened, the assembly met in May.

did his brothers. From the banks of the Rhine he kept watch upon an arc of disturbed and hungry people who were beginning to feel Slav pressure behind them. These were the Danes, Saxons, Thuringians and Bavarians. Fighting them and keeping them at bay, Theuderic and his son Theudebert (modern French Thierry and Thibert) earned a name that lived on in Germanic epic, and established the right of the Franks to watch over the movements of tribes in the heart of Germany, to intervene forcibly in tribal vendettas, and to exact, when they could, heavy tribute of livestock and slaves.

Theudebert, in particular, was a figure of European importance; for, apart from his northern campaigns, he was to some extent concerned in the destruction of the Gothic Mediterranean empire by the Emperor Justinian. He sent more than one expedition into northern Italy and was certainly in correspondence with Byzantium. We must not make too much of this by supposing that Byzantium already foresaw and approved the rise of the Frankish empire, though in using the Catholic Franks as a counter-balance to the Arian Goths Byzantium was at least admitting the arrival of a new force in western politics. Nor must we think of Frankish Catholicism as permanently established. Both the sons and grandsons of Clovis appear to have played with the Arianism of the more highly romanized Visigoths; and Gregory certainly regarded Arianism as a very present danger—and perhaps as a more serious threat to the Catholic hierarchy than the wayward savagery of the Frankish chieftains; for savagery, as Gregory understood it, was easily forgivable when directed, as by Clovis and Theudebert, into suitable channels. If the battle between Catholicism and Arianism was still not quite over, that between Christianity and paganism certainly was—except, of course, in the depths of the countryside. The Franks had no hesitation in bringing their thank-offerings to the shrines of the miracle-working Gaulish saints, such as St. Martin, under whom they won their battles and amassed their treasures; and no sense of moral obloquy or incongruity pursued them when they left the shrines to cut the throats of unloved kinsmen. It is not their fault but Gregory's—who could not even speak their language—if they have come down to us as hopelessly immoral and utterly unconcerned with the welfare of Gaul.

The feuds, the *bella civilia*, that so horrified Gregory are difficult to follow and cannot be gone into here. But it is, nevertheless, possible to follow them and to sort out many of the motives that inspired them. They were fought at great cost—the harrying of good land (notably church land), the destruction of buildings, and perhaps the maiming of Gallo-Roman commerce and culture. But destruction was not the aim of the Franks: they had inherited what they could hardly understand and thus could not be expected to preserve. Not unintelligent, they continued to live their own lives under the critical and unsympathetic gaze of the Gallo-Romans, until the day came when the two were no longer distinguishable.

With the end of the sixth century, Frankish history seems to enter a new phase; for Gregory of Tours is dead. For narrative sources we must turn to the so-called chronicle of Fredegarius, the work of several hands, perhaps Burgundian, but only independent of Gregory from the year 584; to the *Liber Historiae Francorum*, a Neustrian chronicle, which is of value from the mid-seventh century; and to the Lives, Passions and Miracles of Saints which we owe to the literary tradition established by Gregory the Great as well as to the independent tradition of the Irish monks who reached Gaul at about this time. The greatest of these, St. Columbanus of Luxeuil and Bobbio, lives in the pages of a fine biography by Jonas of Susa. The volume of such writings is considerable and their value high. Yet they lack Gregory's fire and are often enough ill-written.

But do they really reveal a new political scene? Are the Merovingian kings of the seventh century pursuing objects unknown to their predecessors? They rule, of course, over a more closely integrated society the economic position of which has undergone change, and the faith of which is safely Catholic; but the political unification of Gaul is no more of an objective than it had ever been, and historians waste time in arguing that it could be. Sometimes a single Merovingian, the only survivor of his generation, rules over all Gaul. (Apart from assassination, the royal house was already suffering from that physical degeneracy which led to its eclipse.) But when he does, he moves seldom beyond the royal estates of the part of Gaul that is his fatherland, and is content to leave the remainder in the hands of local magnates. Thus, Chlotar II (584–629), a Neustrian, made no attempt to bend the Austrasian Franks to his will but left them in virtual independence under a deputy, or Mayor of the Palace. Later, he gave them his small son, Dagobert, to live under the care of the greatest of the Austrasian magnates, Pepin of Landen and Arnulf of Metz (the forebears of the Carolingian dynasty), well knowing that he would grow up to identify himself with Austrasian interests.

Dagobert, like Clovis, was a special favourite of the Church, and in particular of the Abbey of St. Denis, near Paris. The fortunes of the French monarchy were to be closely intertwined with those of the great monastery. They grew up together. St. Denis, first bishop of Paris, had been martyred in the middle of the third century. The local cult of the saint was firmly established by the end of the fifth century. In the following century it spread over Gaul, and St. Denis gained a reputation as the protector of animals and of those in danger of their lives. By the early seventh century, pilgrims from outside Gaul were regularly visiting the shrine for the celebration of the saint's day (9th October). Dagobert was not the first of his dynasty to show an interest in the cult and to extend his protection over the community's lands and possessions; but he did show it special favour by richly embellishing the church with gold and gems (perhaps under the supervision of his treasurer and goldsmith, St. Eloi, later bishop of Noyon); and he did grant a charter for the holding of an annual fair on the occasion of the October celebrations. It should be added that the community was a loosely connected fraternity of clerics and laymen living under the rule of St. Martin, and did not become a Benedictine house, with the privilege of immunity from episcopal jurisdiction, till the latter part of the seventh century.

Many medieval fairs originated in some form of religious festival. The fair of St. Denis was probably only intended as a market of provisions for the large number of pilgrims, and to begin with would have been largely confined to the trading of winter provisions. But the occasion for further trade was so propitious that the fair grew rapidly in importance until it became a main source of the vast wealth of the abbey. Northern merchants with their furs and wool came from England and Scandinavia to barter with the southerners bringing wine and honey. It is this kind of activity that suggests that, as the Dark Ages advanced, the Mediterranean-facing trade of Roman Europe was giving way to a trade with its centre of gravity in the North. But it is unwise to press this too far, since, on the one hand Mediterranean trade of the sixth and seventh centuries is ill-documented, and on the other, archaeologists are increasingly disposed to see evidence of considerable, if spasmodic, trade from the Levant in Frankish Gaul during the same period. The trouble was not that goods such as spices and papyrus from the Levant were unobtainable in Gaul, nor that they were unwelcome, but simply that the Franks had nothing to export in return, except arms and slaves. Hence the balance of trade was heavily against the West, and the drain of gold to the East was increasingly burdensome, at least until the monetary reforms of the Carolingian age. This state of affairs was only exacerbated by Vandal and later by Arab activities in the Mediterranean.

That the Merovingians inherited a land still rich in gold is certain; indeed, it was a contributory factor in their decision to move south. In taking over the imperial domains (or *fiscus*) as their own, they took over also a tradition of taxation which their retainers neither understood nor approved. Gregory of Tours gives several instances of Frankish resistance to increasingly heavy re-assessments, which resistance was due probably less to a belief that taxation was unjustifiable because unproductive (i.e. the Merovingians but not the state benefited) than to a much older belief that the proper way for kings to replenish their treasure-hoards was by plunder-raids outside their own territories. Such raids were frequently undertaken, to Italy, Spain and elsewhere; for example, Dagobert in a single raid on Spain made 200,000 gold *solidi*; but their yield was insufficient. Meanwhile, in addition to plunder and taxes, the Merovingians could count on occasional large subsidies from Byzantium and on the still more occasional release of pagan temple-treasures. Thus, at least till Dagobert's time, Merovingian gold coinage was plentiful and not subject to fluctuations in weight. It was a vigorous coinage, indicative of a busy commercial life.

Since the sixth century, the sea-borne trade of the north-west had been increasingly in the hands of the Frisians. Their ships were active between England, Scandinavia, Gaul and even further afield. Already in Dagobert's time they frequented the fairs of St. Denis, perhaps bringing with them their most characteristic article of trade, lengths of Frisian cloth, or *pallia Fresonica*, the wool for which may well have been bought in the markets of London or York. At Duurstede, near the mouth of the Rhine, Dagobert sited a mint to help finance this trade; from his time, or soon after, silver begins to replace gold as the favoured metal for northern coinage. Gallic silver coin-hoards, including many Anglo-Saxon silver *sceattas*, of the century after Dagobert betray the presence of Anglo-Frisian traders deep in Frankish territory and notably along the Rhine. It was here, at such towns as Mainz, that the northern traders made contact with the old Gallo-Roman trading communities, and met the southerners who had crossed the Alps and come up the valley of the Rhine, or sometimes up the Rhône, with their Mediterranean goods. It has been argued that certain new artistic influences were now reaching the North by passing along this route rather than through Provence or Aquitaine; but such evidence is difficult to use objectively, and the truth seems to be that no one trade-route ever long enjoyed an undisturbed monopoly in the Dark Ages.

The intrinsic value of the Frisian trade and the dues that could be levied on it at the ports explain the interest shown by Dagobert and his successors in the area of the Rhine mouth. Here they were prepared to construct strong-points, notably at Utrecht, and to encourage missionary work among the pagan, and often rebellious, Frisians. Both the Irish and the Bene-dictines took part in the dangerous work of conversion, which advanced hand-in-glove with Frankish political and com-mercial control. A just appreciation of the value of the Rhine trade will also help to explain Dagobert's determination to defend the Austrasian Franks from the menace of the Avars.

The Avars were a group of mounted nomadic tribes related to the Huns, and sharing their courage and ferocity. Driven

westward by the Turks from their Caspian homeland, they had
settled in Pannonia and made it the heart of a formidable
empire. From the time of their first brush with the Franks,
in 562, they proved a continual threat to the security of the
tribes living under Frankish protection east of the Rhine.
Several Merovingians fought with them or bought them off.
Dagobert managed to unite not only the Franks but also the
Germans in resistance, and in particular made use of a Saxon
offer of help, which secured the Rhineland for the rest of his
reign. The Saxons' price was the cancellation of an annual
tribute of 500 cows which the Franks had been accustomed to
exact from them. Contemporaries were enormously impressed
by what Dagobert had done: he was one of the great Frankish
heroes, who held his lands against the eastern hordes. Men as
far distant as the Bavarians sought his overlordship and
obtained it.

Dagobert died in January, 639, and was buried (like most
of his successors) in the abbey church of St. Denis. He was
thirty-six. We know—what contemporaries did not know—that
he was to be the last of the great Merovingian kings. He had the
ruthless energy of a Clovis and the cunning of a Charlemagne.
By accident he had come to be the only ruler over all the Franks,
and had thus imposed on them, at a formative period in their
history, a personal, unitary rule. But to speak of the Frankish
State making a last stand against the forces of disruption is
beside the point. Dagobert did not expect to pass on his rule
undivided to a single heir. He knew well that Austrasian and
Neustrian Franks (to say nothing of Aquitanians and Burgundians) had widely divergent interests and felt no love for
each other. And thus he left Austrasia to his son Sigebert (to be
brought up by Austrasians) and Neustria and Burgundy to a
younger son, Clovis. Dagobert moved, through a long reign,
in the ways of his fathers.

When copying out Gregory's account of the nuptials of
Clovis's parents, Childeric and Basina, Fredegarius inter-
polated a story of his own, to the effect that on their wedding
night, Basina thrice sent Childeric outside to bring her news of
whatever he should see. The first time he reported lions and
leopards; the second, bears and wolves; the third, lesser

beasts, such as dogs. "And so", said Basina, "shall your descendants be". Whether personal animus or popular tradition lay behind this tale, Fredegarius was expressing no more than the truth. The Merovingian successors of Dagobert were lesser beasts. Even when we allow for the extreme difficulty of interpreting the surviving records—and allow, too, for the probability that the early Carolingians did what they could to damage the reputation of those they supplanted—the fact remains that the later Merovingians were *rois fainéants*, sluggards, not warriors, the race in whom (in Einhard's phrase) there was no more vigour. They remained at home, taking we know not what part in the life of their people, pottering round their estates on their ox-waggons. The remarkable fact is that, alone of the barbarian dynasties, their royal blood retained a sacrosanct quality long after they had ceased to be warriors. The Merovingians of the seventh and eighth centuries lived, on the whole, shorter lives than their predecessors. Some died by assassination, but more died in boyhood, or soon after, from natural causes. They were physical degenerates.

Somehow, therefore, it is nearly impossible not to think of seventh-century Gaul in terms of a steady decline in royal power, and of an equally steady rise in aristocratic, and notably of Arnulfing, power. Historians are fascinated by the contrast, seeing, as they must, the end of the story—the seizure of royal power by the Arnulfing Mayors of the Palace, the descendants of Pepin of Landen and Arnulf of Metz. But the Arnulfings cannot have seen things thus. They cannot have seen the progressive degeneracy of the Merovingians, nor that the papacy would one day help them by covering their terrible lack of royal blood with a different veneer of sacrosanctity. There was no *mouvement ascensionnel de la dynastie*.

The Arnulfings drew their strength from the land. They farmed rich estates in the Ardennes and Brabant, of which two —Landen and Herstal—gave their names to members of the family. It may well be that there were other magnates, Austrasian and Neustrian, with estates as extensive; but the future was less concerned to preserve their memory. The Arnulfings, at all events, were doing nothing very extraordinary when they used their improving fortunes to found and endow religious communities, as at Nivelles, St. Hubert and Andenne. Here, the ladies of the family, such as Gertrude and Begga, could pass their days in comfort, and family treasure and deeds could be stored. The rise of innumerable small religious houses is similarly related to the fortunes of aristocratic families; and naturally, the memory of such founders and protectors was cherished over the centuries. We may go further and say that, in the case of the Arnulfings, such foundations were intimately connected with the activities of Irish and Roman missionaries. St. Amand was one who worked under their patronage.

The hatred of Austrasians for Neustrians, and the anxiety of each to avoid control by the other, is a more significant feature of Frankish life than any supposed attempt of the magnates to diminish the power of their kings. Between the two peoples lay a belt of rich marcher-land, notably in the neighbourhood of Reims, over which disputes arose. The complicated feuds of the fifty years after Dagobert's death, with Merovingians and Mayors of the Palace flitting across the stage in apparent confusion, are a good deal concerned with these lands, and with the claims upon them not of states (for Neustria and Austrasia were hardly that) but of families and churches. An engagement of more than usual importance was the battle of Tertry (near St. Quentin) where, in 687, the Austrasians, under Pepin II, routed the Neustrians. This defeat, and the eclipse of the Neustrian Mayors, marked the effective end of the old Merovingian centre of power, and permitted the Arnulfing Mayors to intervene at will in Neustrian politics. But the Merovingian kings continued.

One very characteristic royal function Pepin II now assumed: that of defending Francia from external attack. In the first place, after years of fighting, he pushed back the Frisians from the area of Utrecht and Duurstede, entered into a family alliance with their king, Radbod, and installed an Englishman, Willibrord, in Utrecht, to direct missionary operations. A significant aspect of this co-operation was their joint reliance upon Rome. Thus, partly with English assistance, the Arnulfings' early interest in the Irish missionaries developed naturally into an alliance with the Roman church. Pepin also led expeditions against eastern neighbours who were becoming restive—the Alamanni, the Franconians[1] and the Bavarians. Again, one encounters the active co-operation of Irish and Roman missionaries and is reminded that the hostility of the two churches was of short duration.

The Neustrian *Liber Historiae Francorum* closes its account of Pepin's life with this simple phrase "at that time (i.e. Dec. 714) Pepin fell sick of a fever and died. He had held rule under the above-mentioned kings for twenty-seven and one-half years". He had neither obtained, nor aimed at, a crown, which, if might were right, he could so easily have done. He had shown in battle, and the church had admitted it, that his great estates entitled him to have things his own way. Yet he had nothing new to leave to his depleted family but the right to exercise a very chancy supervision over the great men of Francia. And he had no better means than had the Merovingians of ensuring a peaceful succession to his goods. The perpetual re-adjustment of family claims was still the business of life; and consequent vendettas were not an admission of social decay.

Pepin's effective successor was an illegitimate son, Charles Martel. He is the first member of his family to bear the name of Charles, from which they eventually became known as Carolingians. He is a figure of myth as well as of history, round whom the medieval *jongleurs* wove their stories; so that to disentangle his deeds and even his reputation from those of other Charleses is not always easy. He must concern us here as one who vigorously carried on whatever his father had left unfinished. The greatest Austrasian landowner, his chief concern was to protect the north-east of Francia, and the Frankish territory of Hesse and Thuringia, east of the Rhine, from restive neighbours: Neustrians, Frisians, Saxons, and, more remotely, Bavarians. The punitive expeditions to which this policy gave rise struck the imagination of contemporaries: they were the work of a true chieftain, a king, and were, perhaps, the cause rather than the result of a period of comparative quiet among the Franks at home.

Two great missionaries helped Charles to pacify and settle

[1]That is, Franks living east of the Rhine, in what was to become the German Duchy of Franconia.

the periphery of his world. One was his father's friend, Willibrord, and the other a second Englishman, St. Boniface. The northern Frisians, living between the Zuider Zee and the lower Weser, clung to their heathenism till Charlemagne's forced conversion of the Saxons removed their last support. Between 719 and 739 Willibrord continued his labours, largely from Utrecht, where the Arnulfings endowed his church with a good deal of property. But his special home was Echternach, near Trier, in the heart of Rhenish Austrasia. Conceivably Willibrord may have organized from Echternach the earliest missionary work among the tribes east of the Rhine, though the chief credit for this must go to St. Boniface.

Like Willibrord, St. Boniface derived strength from reliance upon the papacy. He visited Rome three times. On the first occasion he assumed the name of Boniface (that of a Roman martyr) and received a commission to preach to the heathen; on the second, he was consecrated bishop and made a profession of obedience to St. Peter; and on the third he became archbishop of the church of the Germans—a new ecclesiastical province. His work made slow progress, however. Partly, this may have been due to the hostility of other bishops of the Rhineland; but, in the main, it was simply that the Germans themselves clung passionately to their heathen gods, and rightly identified the advance of Frankish overlordship with the death of heathenism. The method favoured by Boniface, and approved by Rome, was the establishment of Benedictine houses as centres for teaching and preaching. Such were Amöneburg, Fritzlar and Ohrdruf. The monks lived on the land where they settled, and accordingly cleared forest and waste for their own use. This attracted peasant settlements in the same areas, and so virgin soil came increasingly into cultivation, and the Germans lost what remained of their primitive awe of the forest depths in which the tribal gods had lived undisturbed. The needs of the missionary churches and the tribal craving for land were together satisfied. The monks were the driving force behind the whole colonizing movement—farmers and traders, financiers and builders, physicians, teachers and priests.

In southern Germany, something resembling ecclesiastical

organization already existed, and had existed since the Later Empire. There were bishoprics at Bâle, Constance, Chur and Augsburg, and important monasteries at Reichenau (on an island in Lake Constance) and at Murbach. The last were the foundation of Pirmin, a Visigothic exile befriended by Charles Martel. No bishoprics survived in Bavaria. But there were monasteries at Regensburg, Freising, Salzburg and Passau; and these four became the centres of diocesan organization. It must be emphasized that here, as in central Germany, the work of the first bishops was successful just in so far as account was taken of tribal matters and the co-operation of the chieftains was obtained. But all this work was a mere beginning; the surface of paganism had scarcely been scratched, and huge areas, such as Saxony, were untouched and hostile. However, St. Boniface had made a vital contribution towards something which nature had not intended—the unification of Germany.

Within the old Frankish lands, Charles kept a firm hold on the church and its great men. The line between lay and ecclesiastical magnates was not clear. They were of the same blood and felt equally the call of family feuds. Their lands lay side by side and were often hard to distinguish. So Charles treated all his magnates alike. Where he seemed to go beyond custom was in his treatment of ecclesiastical property. His habit was to confiscate church lands as and when he required them for his warriors. The extent, and even the effect, of these confiscations is not known. The church naturally objected to the loss of revenue involved; but its lands were very extensive, and Charles, like many other barbarian kings (including King Alfred), had no option but to take what he needed. The old imperial lands in Gaul, the *fiscus* inherited by Clovis, had long since been squandered in gifts by the Merovingians; indeed, this was one of the chief reasons for their growing political weakness. The subsequent decline of the Frankish church is often laid at the door of Charles Martel. But it is difficult to prove a connection between the loss of lands and revenue and the spread of clerical indiscipline.

Nor must it be thought that Charles was indifferent to the support of the church. He relied much on the great religious communities, like St. Denis, and made gifts to them. In one case at least, there is interesting evidence of a church in Marseilles to which he actually restored property. He was as credulous as every other Frank and would no doubt always have preferred endowment to extortion. In fact, he practised both.

Charles Martel's military requirements were heavy. His ceaseless campaigning meant the upkeep of a great host of warriors. These warriors were for the most part rewarded with lands, there being insufficient money to pay them in cash for their services. Some historians hold that these grants of land were specifically intended to enable the recipients to provide troops of armed horsemen for the host, and that one at least of the constituent elements of what we call feudalism was thus born. This view is connected with the belief that the new emphasis on cavalry was forced on Charles by his enemies in southern Gaul. These enemies were the Arab and Berber invaders from Africa, who had conquered Visigothic Spain almost as an afterthought and had then advanced over the Pyrenees to raid at will among the cities of Septimania and Aquitaine. A raiding force of this kind, bound perhaps for Tours, was met and beaten by Charles in the *suburbium* of Poitiers in October 732. A Spanish chronicler, the Pseudo-Isidore, writing a generation later, said that the Arab cavalry broke against the Franks as against a wall of ice; and certainly the victory was impressive. Medieval men liked to compare it with the more important defence of Constantinople against the same foe by the Emperor Leo III in 717. The battle of Poitiers was only one incident in the long business of expelling the Arabs from southern Gaul, and of persuading the local nobility not to regard them as better overlords than the Arnulfings. But it was won *Christo auxiliante* and did much for the repute of the Arnulfing dynasty.

But did the Arabs fight on horseback? Recent research in Moslem sources has revealed that the first regular cavalry squadrons did not arrive from Africa till eight years after the battle of Poitiers, and even then fought their first engagements on foot. Both Arab and Frankish cavalry were slow to develop thereafter. It is possible that we shall have to learn to dissociate Charles Martel's land-grants from his alleged need for horsemen and to see the beginnings of that process somewhat later, when his heirs had to face the cavalry not of the Arabs but of the Lombards, the Frisians and the Basques.

In 737 the Merovingian Theuderic IV died, leaving no heir. For four years Charles lived without a king and without himself making the slightest attempt to become one. He divided the lands he ruled between his two sons, being no more bothered than any other Frank about the unity of the *Regnum Francorum*. Carloman was given Austrasia, Alamannia and Thuringia; and Pepin III Neustria, Burgundy and Provence. Aquitaine and Bavaria were left to their own devices: only a Merovingian could dispose of them. A recent historian has written of Charles that "in extinguishing and breaking every autonomy that threatened to weaken the central power, he had saved the unity of the Frankish monarchy". But the same writer then goes on to say that "the accession of the sons of Charles Martel to power was marked by a general revolt in all the outlying parts of the state". In other words, we are more or less back where we were before. By attributing modern motives to these Frankish chieftains, from Clovis to Charles Martel, we make each in turn look ridiculous. What distinguishes Charles from other great men of the late Merovingian period is not his views about kingship, nor his reactions to Frankish domestic problems, the church, the distant German tribes or even the Arabs, but his heroic vigour. He had some of the qualities of a Beowulf, and stood nearer to that heroic figure than to the administrator-kings of the Middle Ages.

CHAPTER V

THE FRANKS (2)

THERE is more to be learned from their contemporaries about the Carolingian kings than about the Merovingian, and one is no longer left to the mercy of a single and largely uncorroborated narrative, like that of Gregory of Tours, for information about a long period of history. Why this should have come about is less easy to determine than might at first appear, for it involves consideration not simply of the increase in literary output and the multiplication of records by the Carolingians, but also of Carolingian willingness to falsify the Merovingian record, and finally of an understandable medieval preference for whatever was Carolingian at the expense of whatever was Merovingian. So it is not enough to say (what is true) that there were better opportunities for writing in the later period than in the earlier, and that the Carolingian world was politically more stable than the Merovingian.

The Frankish state and way of life underwent no change on the day when the first Carolingian supplanted the last Merovingian as king. But for the Carolingians the change was very great, and the realization of this is reflected in the literary and other evidence that we must now consider. Their supporters saw the Carolingians as new priest-kings whose security would turn not upon a severely traditional outlook like that of their predecessors but upon a fresh, consistent and plausible interpretation of the past. History, legend, law, letters and the arts could be bent to the glorification of the new line of kings; and so, to some extent, they were. The purpose of this chapter will be to consider the early Carolingian kings in the light of this view of our sources.

What are our sources? First, in the field of historical narrative (that is, of chronicles) the two main Merovingian sources, the continuation of Fredegarius and the *Liber Historiae Francorum*, come to an end. The last continuator of Fredegarius betrays Arnulfing patronage when he writes, under the fateful year 751, "up to this point, the illustrious Count Childebrand, uncle of king Pepin, caused this history or *gesta* of the Franks to be recorded with the greatest care. But from now on the authority is the illustrious Nibelung, son and successor of Childebrand". This is, in brief, a family history, and we must not look for objective scholarship. However, the chronicle was discontinued from 768, and its place is taken by the more strictly monastic annals—that is, by the extended use of yearly entries of important events in the lunar calendars which the church originally drew up in order to calculate the date of Easter.[1] The origin and relationship of the various Frankish annals are still far from being settled, but the most important are the Royal annals, of which one scholar has written "they have the king as their central figure, and they chronicle his campaigns and the chief measures of his government". Without these annals, our knowledge of the history and chronology of the Carolingians would be seriously impaired.

Based upon the annals are certain biographies. (They are quite distinct from the *Lives of Saints*, which continue to form a vital part of Frankish literature.) The first of these is Einhard's *Life of Charlemagne*, written in the difficult days that followed the Emperor's death. Einhard knew Charlemagne and his family intimately and we must accept his work as well-informed. All the same, the Life is, in addition, a political tract closely modelled on Suetonius' *Lives of the Twelve Caesars*. It is impossible to determine how much of the real Charlemagne Einhard wished to portray or how seriously his text became corrupted in transmission. But how could he be expected to fit his barbarian hero into the mould of classical biography without violating truth? Einhard wrote for the present, not for the future; and we should remember this when we take—as we must—our Carolingian history from him.

Much correspondence has survived. There is, for example, the correspondence of St. Boniface, some of it with the papacy.

[1] These should be distinguished from the solar calendars or martyrologies in which monasteries kept records of annual events like Saints' Days which did not vary with the date of Easter. Thus chronology reinforced the medieval belief in the mutability of all that had to do with the moon and the constancy of whatever depended on the sun.

There is also the great collection of correspondence between the Carolingians and the papacy, put together in the year 791 on Charlemagne's instructions, and known as the *Codex Carolinus*. But there is much else besides, and a good deal can be learnt of men as important as Alcuin and Theodulf and Paul the Deacon from extant letters, many of which were preserved as models for letter-writing.

A word must be said about official sources. They are much fuller than for the earlier Frankish period but they subject the user to a discipline just as severe. Palaeography and diplomatic (i.e. the study of the form of official documents) play their part in rescuing the historian from traps that were never intended for him, though he still falls quite happily into some. Among such documents may be distinguished, first, diplomas. These were official instruments, couched in an elaborate form of words and authenticated in several ways, whereby kings made known their gifts and grants to communities or individuals, and did so in what seemed to them the safest and most permanent manner. There are about forty extant Merovingian diplomas, and many more Carolingian. Thus, a king may announce the grant of an immunity to a religious house, or a right (e.g. to elect an officer), or a confirmation of existing privileges in diplomatic form, on papyrus or parchment. The intention was to impress not just the recipient but also those against whom the recipient and his heirs might later have to defend their right. In spite, however, of all precautions, it was not very difficult for medieval scribes to forge diplomas well enough to deceive rivals; and, since Charlemagne seemed to the Middle Ages the most illustrious of the barbarian heroes, he was also the most popular victim of monasteries (e.g. St. Denis) that wanted to father their threatened privileges on to a donor whose name and memory inspired fear. So there are many bogus diplomas. But what remain uncontaminated form an invaluable collection.

In addition to diplomas there are capitularies. These are ordinances, divided into chapters and representing original legislative activity. Most of them deal with problems of administration affecting public order, the church, the royal domains, the machinery of justice or defence. They tell us little about private, penal or tribal law. Some apply to the whole Frankish world, some only to a part. They are not a codification of custom. They are territorial rather than personal in their application, and are the outcome of the king's discussions of public business with any from whom he might wish to take counsel. Various collections of capitularies were made in the course of the early Middle Ages—collections that contained also tribal laws, legal tracts and excerpts from the annals. They were intended for use in monastic libraries. Thus, the collections in which the Carolingian capitularies survive are in no sense official. They are copies of copies. And so, here again, an important source of information is subject to serious limitation where it cannot be corroborated.

Like the Lombards and Anglo-Saxons, the Franks were interested in tribal law and, moved by the same forces, took pains to write it down. Reference has already been made to the problems presented by the Salian Law. The ninth century was the time when it seemed to evoke a fresh interest. Similarly, the Frankish Ripuarian Law came to be written down, and so also, under Frankish guidance, the Saxon and other Laws. They constituted what could be collected of the whole body of tribal custom by which a Germanic people lived, and their analysis is less advanced than is that of the capitularies and diplomas. They may not, after all, tell us very accurately how the tribes of the immediate post-migration period lived, but they do tell us how the learned men of the Carolingian age thought they had lived, and are thus important in a sense not intended by their compilers. This does not, of course, mean that tribal custom was not still a reality: a well-known letter by Archbishop Agobard of Lyon describes the confusion caused by peoples of different blood choosing to live and be judged by their own customs inside one city. But the natural life of custom tends to petrifaction once it has been committed to writing.

This brief summary only touches some of the written sources from which any account of the Carolingians must be reconstructed. And it quite ignores the archaeological evidence of monumental art and sculpture, and the evidence of the little things, the mosaics, enamels, bronzes, ivories, book-illustrations, in the making of which the Franks were masters. This wealth of material is the substance of the Carolingian renaissance, which is considered below. Not much survives; but what does, is a magnificent gesture towards *Romanitas*.

In the last chapter it was argued that the rise of the Carolingians may have been no more obvious to contemporaries than was the decline of the Merovingians. It is now necessary to go a step further: the *coup d'état*, when it came, was by no means a foregone conclusion, nor even then was it irreversible. The Carolingians were to learn what insecurity meant.

The political fragmentation following upon Charles Martel's death in 741 was of a familiar pattern; and out of disorder and feud emerged another Merovingian. This was Childeric III. The annals say nothing about him, understandably perhaps; but the arresting fact is that the sons of Charles Martel should have had to bother about him at all, and to revive the Merovingian kingship. The blood of Clovis still mattered. Meanwhile, the Arnulfings drew closer to the papacy. This is instanced in the frequency of church councils, both in Austrasia and in Neustria. These councils were great occasions, when secular and ecclesiastical magnates met together. Their decrees give a clear picture of the disorders of the period and of the efforts of responsible men to curb them. They endeavoured, for instance, to provide a regular, unbroken succession in church offices, since long vacancies invited spoliation. To maintain the hierarchy was, at the lowest, a political necessity. The battle with the paganism of the countryside is also reflected in the decrees. The fourth canon of the council of Estinnes, of 743, reads: "we further order, as our father before us ordered, that any person guilty of pagan observances shall be fined 15 *solidi*". Other decrees deal with marriage laws, clerical celibacy, the behaviour of the clergy. Their general tenor is well summarized in the first canon of the Austrasian council of April, 742, known as the *Concilium Germanicum*: "by the advice of my clergy and great men I have provided for bishops in the *civitates* and have placed over them Boniface as archbishop— he who is sent from St. Peter. And I have ordered the yearly calling of a council in which, in my presence, canonical decrees and the laws of the church may be restored and the Christian religion emended. Further, I have restored and given back to the churches revenues wrongly taken from them; and I have removed, degraded and forced penance upon false priests and adulterous deacons and *clerici*." It is Carloman who speaks, Charles Martel's elder son, *dux et princeps Francorum*; but behind him stand the missionaries of the Anglo-Saxon church; and behind them, Rome.

Carloman fell increasingly under the influence of the church, so that in the summer of 747 he abdicated his power in favour of his brother Pepin, ruler of Neustria, and retired to Monte Cassino to become a monk. This left Pepin the sole effective ruler over all the lands of the Franks—over all, that is, where he could enforce his power. But this had not been his father's plan; it was an accident.

Pepin does not seem to have shared his brother's enthusiasm for St. Boniface, possibly because the problem of the restitution of church lands was more complicated in Neustria than in Austrasia. But the more papal influence grew in his dominions the more anomalous his position, as Mayor of the Palace, was likely to seem. In 746 he consulted Pope Zacharius about the powers of metropolitans. The Pope replied at great length and took occasion to compare Pepin with Moses. In 750 Pepin sent two messengers (one, the abbot of St. Denis) to Rome. They were to enquire whether it was right that a ruler enjoying no power should continue to bear the title of king. The Pope replied that it was not right. The separation of the function and the title of ruler was as alien to Roman as to Germanic tradition. The whole practice of rule as based on the Bible and expounded by Rome was against the anomaly so long countenanced by the Franks. But apart from these considerations, the papacy, with its mounting fear of the Lombards, could no more afford to cross the Arnulfings than the Arnulfings could afford to throw off the ecclesiastical power under which they had grown up. The Merovingian Childeric III was no feebler than his predecessors and might easily have prolonged his dynasty. He had a son. When the two were shorn of their locks (scalped, possibly) and shut up in the Abbey of St. Bertin in November, 751, they had been forcibly and publicly dispossessed of their heritage to make way for the Arnulfings.

There must be no doubt about it: the Merovingians did not
peter out but were violently displaced. And it was Rome that
pushed Pepin over the precipice that otherwise he might not
even have seen. The Arnulfings, or the Carolingians as we
should now call them, were kings at the instance of Rome, and
to make them more so they were ritually anointed in a way in
which no Merovingian had ever been.[1] Samuel had anointed
David king in the place of Saul, and so the church, aware of
the parallel, anointed Pepin and his successors. The Franks
were the Chosen of the Lord, their armies the columns of
Israel. The process of identification of the Old Testament figure
of David, the *Christus Domini*, with the Carolingian ruler must
have been simple to a church that had succeeded in identifying
the popes with the New Testament figure of St. Peter. Only
those as saturated in Biblical study as were the men of the
Middle Ages could hope to grasp the vivid relevance of such
parallels.

The papal-Frankish correspondence covering this period is
nearly all elaborated and dressed up in Biblical language. So
equally are the valuable biographies of the contemporary popes
collected together in the *Liber Pontificalis*. The difficulty is
to see the Franks themselves behind the men of learning.

In January, 754, Pope Stephen II reached the royal villa
at Ponthion on the Marne. He had come, perhaps with Byzantine approval, to seek the Franks' help in Italy; for King
Aistulf was threatening the Roman *ducatus* itself. Pepin undertook to restore the exarchate as well as the rights and properties
of the *Respublica Romanorum* seized by Aistulf. Very probably
the pope had brought with him from Rome, and produced
at this juncture, the famous *Constitutum Constantini*, the
donation of Constantine to Pope Silvester I of sovereignty over
the West. The donation, which only survives in a ninth-
century copy, is in one sense a forgery. But its object was to
prove in writing privileges that the author may have believed
to be authentic.[2] On its authority Pope Stephen proceeded to

[1] I leave out of account the fact that the Carolingians were related by
marriage to the Merovingians since it did not seem to strike contemporaries
as important or relevant to the succession.

[2] Another view is that the forgery was committed on the occasion of the
coronation of Louis the Pious by the Pope at Reims in 816.

confer on Pepin and his two sons the title of patrician, formerly
borne by the Exarch of Ravenna and the Duke of Rome. He
further reanointed the family at St. Denis and strictly forbade
the choice of any future king not of the blood of this family
that had been exalted by divine mercy and confirmed and
consecrated by the hand of the Vicar of the Apostles. Thus
Pepin had done all he could to secure some veneer of legality
for his *coup d'état*, and in return opened negotiations with the
Lombards.

These negotiations failed. The subsequent expeditions of
Pepin and his successors across the Alps into Italy were not
lightly undertaken. The Merovingians, indeed, had made the
same journey many times in the past and had usually come back
with much treasure. But it was a hazardous undertaking, and
the newly-established Carolingians certainly disliked commit-
ments so far from home, even when they did mean returning
multis thesauris ac multis muneribus, with much booty and many
gifts. It is incorrect, then, to suppose that Pepin felt any urge
to intervene in Italian affairs. Italy was never quite the magnet
to the Frankish kings that it was to be to the Ottonians.

In Italy, and in Germany also, Pepin seemed to his contemporaries to do less glorious deeds than his son Charlemagne.
His own particular claim to distinction lay in his Aquitanian
campaigns. Southern Gaul had attracted the Franks since the
days of Clovis; whenever they could, they enforced their
suzerainty over it. It was worth plundering, and not less
because the Arabs had come to settle there. It took Pepin
seven years of fighting and negotiation, from 752 to 759, to
establish his authority over Septimania, which he did with
the help of the Visigothic population. The last Arab stronghold
to fall was Narbonne, again with the help of the inhabitants,
who had Pepin's promise that, when liberated, they should
continue to live under Visigothic Law. The siege of Narbonne
was a great affair, as the later *chansons de geste* witness, and it
opened up the whole South as far as the river Ebro. But an
unforeseen result of the overthrow of Arab power in Septimania
was to alarm the Aquitanians, who revolted. Frankish penetration of Aquitania was a slow business. The Aquitanians were
loyal to their duke, and he in his turn was a determined fighter

who could call for help upon the Basques, fine horsemen, and among the best fighters of the Middle Ages. Pepin died while directing final operations from Saintes. He had dealt with Aquitanian separatism more thoroughly than any Merovingian, though he had done it in precisely their spirit. And he ruled in Narbonne and Nîmes.

France was not 'united' by these long campaigns, and it is doubtful if Pepin would have understood what we understand by the word. But he had made the Carolingian power felt in the South, and might have done so still more effectively if rebellions in Germany and obligations in Italy had not distracted him. He was an experimental king, an Old Testament king; and the Franks on the whole liked the experiment.

Of his sons and successors one—Carloman—died within three years. The other, Charlemagne, at once dispossessed his nephews, and thus became sole ruler over the Franks.

Many books have been written about Charlemagne. He has always been a hero of western history as well as of romance, and is by no means the least of the Nine Worthies of the world. It would be impossible to present in a few pages an agreed picture of what now seems significant in his long life, or to decide to what extent we can really penetrate behind the Latin evidence to the motives and character of this famous Frank. We must take him as we find him and admit that most of what we need to know for a full picture is missing. What a recent scholar has termed his personality as a statesman does not and probably never did exist.

For the first ten years of his reign Charlemagne was engaged in the traditional war-business of his house, in Germany, Lombardy and the Spanish march. Apart from a scheme to make western Saxony into a permanent defensive march for the protection of Frankish lands, there is nothing to suggest that his ambitions or abilities exceeded those of Pepin or Charles Martel. He had no great plans of conquest but did actively whatever came to his hand to do. This included the acquisition of the Lombard crown, a natural corollary to years of Frankish intervention in Italy. In Spain he blundered badly and only just succeeded in extricating himself from Islam and at Roncevaux from the Basques. This happened in 778, a year of general revolt throughout his lands. No one explanation will cover the coincidence of unrest in Saxony, Aquitaine, Italy and Francia. Some, perhaps, were always prepared to rise against the *parvenu* dynasty, and others to fish in troubled waters. But the mere fact of the absence of the king and his lack of trustworthy lieutenants explains much. In the course of years Charlemagne gathered round him a group of devoted servants, laymen and clerics, his friends and drinking-companions, who constituted his *palatium* and could be trusted to do his business; but this, and the sense of omnipresence that grew with Charlemagne's ceaseless mobility, were slow to come and certainly did not exist in 778. At Herstal, in the following year, the king took certain measures to ensure firmer administration in the Frankish and Lombard kingdoms. We learn from the subsequent capitulary that his counts were to see that justice was done; anyone refusing to accept compensation for a vendetta was to be sent to the king; and nobody was to dare to form an armed band with hostile intent: *de truste faciendo nemo praesumat*. The administrative machinery by which the royal will was to be enforced is interesting but of less moment than the political revelation that in the eleventh year of Charlemagne's reign the Franks were as unruly as ever.

With the end of the crisis of 778 Charlemagne entered upon the great central period of his career, which lasted till 791. This was the time of military conquest and of the rapid development of his sense of Christian mission. The two went hand in hand. Notable features of the military conquest were the absorption of the great duchy of Bavaria into the Frankish kingdom—an inevitable step since the collapse of Bavaria's neighbour, Lombardy—and the occupation of the southern slopes of the Pyrenees. Charlemagne was surrounding the Franks with a deep belt of marcher territories. However, one result of the absorption of Bavaria was that the Franks found themselves in contact with the terrible Avar horsemen who dominated the Slav peoples of the Middle Danube.

But Charlemagne's greatest undertaking in this period was the subjugation of the Saxons and eastern Frisians. The latter, whom all archaeologists do not agree in distinguishing from the Saxons, were fierce pagans though at the same time good farmers, traders and seamen. Among them, in the area between the Zuider Zee and the Weser estuary, Frankish and Anglo-Saxon missionaries pressed on their work with royal support. Mention should be made of Liudger, himself a Frisian and a disciple of the great missionary school of York. He wrote a biography of his master, Gregory of Utrecht, where he says that when Gregory was dying he distributed among his dependents the books he had once acquired at Rome. Liudger got St. Augustine's *Enchiridion*, thus adding to an already considerable collection made at York. We happen to know that the collection contained a copy of Caedmon's poem, but by and large it must have been strictly utilitarian. The men who converted Northern Europe needed chiefly simple texts, biblical and liturgical, and calendars for determining ecclesiastical chronology; and the dissemination of these was the very substance of what we call the Carolingian Renaissance. In the wake of the missionaries, Frankish counts and other officials penetrated into north-east Frisia, raising contingents for the royal host and doing the other business of secular government. The *Lex Frisionum* remains as a convenient summary of Frisian custom as the Franks of the period understood it. But as with Bavaria so with Frisia: in subjugating a proud and ancient people the Franks had removed the very thing they sought to create—a barrier against enemies much more formidable. Beyond the Frisians lived the Danes.

Since early Merovingian times the Saxons had raided Frankish territory and the Franks had raided the Saxons in reprisal. But the Carolingians had special interests to protect. Their homeland was Austrasia, in the Ardennes, and in the country between the Meuse and the Rhine, rivers that were not barriers but rich trade-routes. Further, the Carolingians had staked their reputation on building up the missionary churches of central Germany, in Hesse and Thuringia. The whole weight of royal interest had shifted towards the Rhine. The richer the Rhineland became the greater became the need to protect its approaches from Saxon raids—and the greater became the difficulty, since beyond the Rhine there was no natural frontier. Frankish writers like Einhard and the annalists were more interested in Charlemagne's Saxon wars than in anything else that he did, for they rightly divined that the fortune of his house was bound up in the protection of the Rhineland.

The central Saxons or Angarians lived along the course of the Weser, with the Eastphalians on one side of them, along the Elbe, and the Westphalians on the other, east of the Rhine. These were the three main divisions of the Saxon people. They had no political cohesion and no need for it, except when threatened as a people. But they did have religious cohesion. They fought to preserve their paganism and its bloodthirsty rites with a tenacity the Franks called obduracy. Their culture and way of life depended on the outcome.

In 772 Charlemagne set out on his first Saxon campaign. It was little more than a reprisal raid of the familiar kind. However, he penetrated deep and garrisoned defence-points beyond and not in the lands he wished to protect. These defence-points were often Saxon fortresses cleverly sited on high ground or at strategic points on the banks of rivers. They must have been centres for trade as well as for resistance to the Franks since Saxon coin-hoards have been found in their vicinity. Not content with this, and with the taking of hostages, Charlemagne also destroyed the Irminsul, the great tree-trunk that supported the heavenly vault for the Saxons. Perhaps he had in mind the precedent of St. Boniface, who had destroyed the Donar Oak at Geismar. Certainly he knew that the subjugation of the Saxons would mean first the suppression of paganism. The destruction of the Irminsul and the subsequent forced mass-baptisms were never forgiven: whenever Charlemagne was far away the Saxons would revolt, destroy the Frankish mission-centres and raid as far as possible into Frankish territory. They found a natural leader in a certain Widukind. He was remembered for centuries in Saxon legend, and even made a new appearance as a Germanic hero under the Nazis. The Franks, too, were much impressed by him. In 782 Charlemagne held his court in Germany, near the source of the Lippe. All the Saxon chieftains except those following Widukind came and did homage to him. Probably they were also baptized, for Charlemagne was in deadly earnest about the extirpation of paganism. The church had filled his mind with the missionary fervour of St. Augustine's *De Civitate Dei* and had placed in his hands a copy of Pope Gregory's letter to Aethelberht of Kent on the subject of racial conversion. His kingly task, and that of his Franks, was to convert the heathen, by fire and sword if necessary.

Later in the year 782, a Frankish army making its way south-east through Saxony was set upon and wiped out by the Saxons. Some important officers were among the killed, including two of Charlemagne's close friends. This was the last straw. The Franks entered Saxony in force. Charlemagne won a victory near Verden and massacred 4500 prisoners, quite possibly as an act of private vengeance.[1] The result, of course, was even more widespread rebellion, which it took three years to suppress. Finally, Widukind surrendered and was baptized, his conqueror standing godfather. Some idea of the relief felt may be had from the Pope's letter of congratulation, in which he says that he has ordered three days of thanksgiving for this great Christian victory. The Rhineland and the East Frankish church were saved. For the Saxons, however, the victory meant still fiercer repression, and the imposition upon them of a church organization that they did their best to negative. Frankish anti-pagan measures recorded for these years give a vivid picture of the power and resilience of ancient Germanic heathenism.

We have noted that the rapid development of Charlemagne's sense of Christian mission was a feature of the central period of his reign. In the *Admonitio Generalis*, the great statement of church policy issued under his name in 789, the needs of his church are summarized in eighty-two articles. The policy must have been what the king personally desired; but (despite Einhard) he was an ignorant man, and all the detailed work was that of his learned clerical friends, who were able to make use of earlierFrankish capitularies as well as of Roman canonical collections. The *Admonitio* ranges over many topics—theological, disciplinary, liturgical, and educational among others. One sees from it how closely integrated the Frankish and Roman

---

[1]One scholar argues that what took place was not execution but deportation, and that scribes later confused the verbs *delocare* (to deport) and *decollare* (to execute).

churches had become in a comparatively short time. The Carolingians may in some respects have turned Francia away from the Mediterranean; but in religion at least they bound her to Rome, and to St. Benedict in particular. The *Admonitio* envisages something Roman—a society, a Christian society, living at peace with itself, united under its king and fearing nothing but injustice. The force of this inspiration must not be minimized. It lighted the handful of learned men who somehow saved barbarian Europe from itself. Article 62 reads: "Let peace, concord and unanimity reign among all Christian people, and the bishops, abbots, counts and our other servants, great and small; for without peace we cannot please God." Once again, the thought of St. Augustine shaped western society. The huge gap between theory and practice, between the concept of peace and the fact of bloodshed, was no more closed by Charlemagne than by any of his successors. Yet he was aware of it.

Article 72 is concerned with cathedral and monastic schools and with the transcription and correction of biblical and liturgical texts used in them; and in this way, modestly and practically, the Carolingian renaissance was born.

It has repeatedly been stated in this book that awareness of the classical heritage and anxiety to preserve it characterized the Western barbarians almost as much as the men of the Late Empire. What then is meant by 'the renaissance' of the eighth and ninth centuries? Of what precisely was there a renaissance? Answers to these questions can only be found if it is borne in mind that learning and good letters were no mere hobbies of the Carolingians and their friends. They were conditions of survival. Furthermore, when we speak of Charlemagne's contribution we are often guilty of a minuteness unwarranted by the evidence. Manuscripts, *objets d'art* and other kinds of material evidence are often difficult to date. The renaissance was a cultural process stretching over more than a century; and thus, for example, what we attribute to Charlemagne may sometimes belong to the reign of his grandson, Charles the Bald.

The literary remains of the Franks of pre-Carolingian times are scarce, but are sufficient to justify the view of most scholars that they reflect a low state of culture. They are unattractive in style, their language being the corrupt but living Latin of everyday speech, and unattractive, though not necessarily difficult, to read. Variety, not uniformity, is the characteristic of Merovingian texts, whether biblical, literary or diplomatic. But the Merovingian world was by comparison with the Carolingian a small one, and so variety may not have seemed a serious demerit.

The Carolingians, and particularly Charlemagne, were concerned to provide a trained clergy to convert and live among Frisians, Saxons, Slavs and Avars, as well as to control the more settled areas of the Frankish world. The monastic and cathedral schools were the instruments of this policy. Clerical instruction urgently needed standardization; otherwise its work would fail outside Francia. Scholars were needed, capable of overhauling the very texts on which missionary enterprise depended: the Bible, the liturgy, the main scriptural commentaries and the books of secular instruction that led up to the study of these. Trained scribes were needed who could copy texts accurately, economically (for writing materials were precious) and in a way that would be intelligible to churchmen of whatever nationality.

Like his father, Charlemagne sought help abroad. First from the Lombards, who, for all their savagery, lived in a country incomparably rich in ancient manuscripts, where the tradition of fine writing had never entirely perished. The Lombard royal court had not been unlearned: how could it have been, under the shadow of Byzantium and Rome? Had not King Cunincpert ordered a certain Master Stephen to put into Latin verse the story of how King Perchtarit his father had pacified northern Italy a century before Charlemagne was born? Alcuin describes how he once attended a public disputation in Lombard Pavia between Peter of Pisa (who later joined the Frankish court) and a Jew named Lullus; while even then Paul the Deacon must have been composing his early poems and collecting material for the Lombard History that he was to put into writing years later in southern Italy. From Italy, Charlemagne recruited Paulinus of Aquileia, Fardulf, Peter of Pisa and Paul the Deacon.

But the vital contribution to the renaissance was Insular—

that is to say, Anglo-Irish. The links binding England and Ireland to the continent in the seventh and eighth centuries were numerous and complicated. The Carolingians were much indebted to the great missionary school of York for the men and the books it sent to them. England in particular had become a clearing-house for books brought from Rome and, indeed, from the whole Italian peninsula. This movement of books and men was reinforced by the English Benedictine missionaries' resolve to keep in touch with Rome at all costs. Roman books reaching Canterbury, Jarrow, York, Malmesbury were there copied for the use of English missionaries abroad; and one great English book, the *Codex Amiatinus*, the oldest complete manuscript of the Vulgate now in existence, was taken from Jarrow to Rome in 716 by the abbot Ceolfrid. So England transported and exported that rarest of commodities, learning, at the time when it was most needed. Wherever English missionaries settled, English manuscripts followed. Some reached the big Frankish monastic libraries like Corbie, Tours and St. Denis, while others went further afield to the missionary centres in the north and east, to such places as Utrecht, Echternach, Mainz, Lorsch, Amorbach, Würzburg, Salzburg, Reichenau and above all, Fulda, the favourite home of St. Boniface and then of a wonderful succession of scholars.

What books? Primarily Biblical and devotional texts, the raw material for teaching; but also secular texts, since without some equipment in the liberal arts it was impossible to proceed far. In his *Divine Institutions* Cassiodorus had urged his monks to cultivate letters as the soundest approach to the scriptures, had insisted on the careful copying of manuscripts, advised them to guard against plausible emendations, told them how to bind and keep their books and even made suggestions for an improved spelling. Cassiodorus was much read in the early Middle Ages; and the missionaries, however much they feared the fatal distraction of heathen letters, listened to his advice and took seriously his exposition of dialectic, the art of arguing or putting your case well. Turning then to Cassiodorus' own masters, Cicero, Priscian, Donatus and others, the monks found their works preserved in manuscripts for the most part earlier than the seventh century. They may not have under-

stood much of what they found, but they were full of awe in
the presence of Antiquity; and they were faithful copyists—
and that in a beautiful script of their own devising, upon which
the type of this book is based.

Alcuin, for a time Charlemagne's intimate, was probably
England's greatest single contribution to the continental
renaissance. There are no surprises about Alcuin. He was a
straightforward exponent of what he found in St. Augustine,
St. Benedict, Cassiodorus and Gregory the Great, and belonged
heart and soul to the Italian tradition transmitted through
Bede and the School of York. What he wished to do was to
transmit a received tradition. And that is what he did do. A
strong echo of this resolve may be caught in Charlemagne's
well-known circular to religious houses on the need to cultivate
letters as the proper introduction to the scriptures—a document
of which Englishmen should not be in ignorance, since the
Würzburg copy (the only nearly contemporary copy) is in the
Bodleian Library at Oxford. But if Alcuin shared his master's
views on education, he had, like others, to pay the penalty of
almost constant attendance at the royal court, where he lived
a far from ascetic life, no doubt hunting and carousing with the
rest. In these unsettling conditions he yet composed textbooks
on the seven liberal arts and earned deserved renown as a
liturgiologist, exegete and hagiographer. He was the author
of a collection of letters which is a primary source for the
period; and he played a leading part, mostly late in life, while
abbot of St. Martin's at Tours, in the revision of the Bible.

This last lay at the heart of the Carolingian renaissance.
The Bibles of the eighth century were infinite in their variant
readings. Some were based on St. Jerome's Latin Vulgate,
others were derived from pre-Jerome Latin versions of the
so-called Itala type. Even the Bibles brought in by the English
missionaries showed serious variations, notably in the Gospels
and Psalms—important parts of the Bible because of their rôle
in the Liturgy. In a general letter, Charlemagne writes: "and
thus, God helping us in all things, we have already caused to
be corrected with all possible care the Books of the Old and
New Testaments, degraded through the ignorance of copyists."
We know that Alcuin played a leading part in this great work

of collation because he says as much in a letter to Charlemagne's sister, Gisla, abbess of Chelles, and again to Charlemagne himself, to whom he sent the revised text as a gift, timed to reach Rome on Christmas Day, 800.

Altogether, if attention is focussed on Biblical studies as the central theme of the Carolingian revival, its other facets fall into their proper places, and one begins to see what is meant by calling it modest and practical, and how innumerable its roots were. This was no New Athens finer than the Old: it was intellectual reform and textual criticism as the indispensable preliminary to the reform of the clergy and to the performance of the *Opus Dei*. Wherever one looks one sees abbeys and cathedrals, libraries and· scriptoria, scholars as different as Theodulf the Spaniard and Dungal the Irishman, busy about the king's business in a most impressive way. What is impressive is the weight of their united achievement in manuscripts and objects that we can still handle. It all looks so purposeful and fits in so well with what the reformers themselves tell us about the all-pervading influence of Charlemagne. And why should we hesitate to accept their picture of the Carolingian renaissance as the right one? Why, above all, should we hesitate to accept Einhard's famous, if contradictory, picture, though it dates from thirty years later?

This is what Einhard wrote. First, he pays a tribute to the king's eloquence and to his ability to express himself as easily in Latin as in his native tongue (actually this is a paraphrase of what Suetonius said of the Roman Emperors). Then he goes on:

"He cultivated the liberal arts most assiduously and heaped honours on those who taught them, holding them in the greatest veneration" (this again is from Suetonius). "In the study of grammar he sat under Peter of Pisa, an old man by then. In other studies his master was Alcuin, nicknamed Albino, a ·deacon like Peter, but a Saxon of Britain by birth and the most learned man of his day. He gave much time to the study of rhetoric, dialectic and, above all, astronomy. He picked up the calculus and showed real aptitude in working out the courses of the stars. Furthermore, he tried to write, and usually placed tablets and sheets of parchment under his pillows so that at odd moments when he was resting he could practise tracing letters. But he took up writing too late and the results were not very good. He was most particular in the observance of the Christian religion"—oddly enough, this too is adapted from Suetonius—"in which he had been brought up since childhood. And at Aix he built a church of extraordinary beauty, embellished with gold and silver and candelabra and balustrades and enormous bronze doors. He had columns and marbles brought from Rome and Ravenna, because he could find them nowhere else. When he was well enough, he always attended services morning and evening and watched carefully to see that all was done properly. Quite often he ordered the sacristans to see that the place was decent. He provided many sacred vessels of gold and silver and enough priestly vestments to make sure that no cleric, however humble, had to appear unrobed. Finally, he gave much attention to correct reading and psalmody; for he was an expert, although he never read in public, and sang only in unison or to himself."

Now, most if not all aspects of the Carolingian revival are alluded to by Einhard in this passage. It is not, however, the details of the picture that matter—some of them may have had no foundation in fact—but the impression the author leaves us of a barbarian king whom all sought to magnify, who in his day had shown a capacity for appropriation equalled by very few. An ignorant warrior (for we should not take Einhard's stylized description literally) he had drawn upon all parts of the civilized west for his scholars and artists. They had come to him and worked under his protection. The laws and doctrine of the Roman church were at last safe in barbarian Europe. After all, Rome had been justified in anointing a new race of kings.

But Charlemagne's concern for culture did not mean that he and his family were safe in their subjects' esteem. Indeed, in the midst of his reforms he had to face a series of grave rebellions that brought to a sharp close the central period of his reign. 792 and 793 were terrible years. In the first place, there were bad harvests and widespread famine. Secondly, there was trouble in Saxony, Italy and Spain. And finally, a conspiracy against the king (not the first) almost succeeded in its object. It was led by the king's favourite bastard, Pepin the Hunchback, and involved many of the Frankish magnates. We must not, then, imagine that the protection of the church placed Charlemagne above the vendettas of his race and class. He was still one of a very small circle of barbarian chieftains who quarrelled fiercely among themselves for land or treasure and who were commonly despised outside their own territory.

Much interest and importance for the future attach to the king's measures to avert a repetition of this *magnum conturbium* among his own kindred and in his own circle. How could he tie men more closely to himself? After the earlier conspiracy of 786 he had exacted an oath of allegiance from all his subjects. Such oaths had been normal under the Merovingians, but after the change of dynasty there seems to have been an unwillingness to risk their enforcement. However, after the anointing in 751, Pepin III took an oath of fidelity from his magnates and prefaced it with an act of commendation.

Fidelity, or fealty, is a difficult, vague word. In general, it expressed the trust that men placed in each other: it made living together possible. That is why loyalty to one's oath was counted the greatest of virtues by all barbarians. Further, fealty implied a relationship between men that could be entered into and equally got out of. Under the Merovingians you could always change your master. In a more particular sense, fealty was the personal bond holding every Frank to his king. A Frank who had not taken his oath of fealty might well claim that he could not be guilty of infidelity if he revolted against his lord; and in fact this was claimed by the younger conspirators in 792, and resulted in rigorous orders that all men were to give or renew their oaths in the presence of the king's representatives. Here is an example of an oath of fealty:

"I promise that, from this day forward, I will be the most faithful man of the most pious Emperor, my lord Charles, son of King Pepin and Queen Bertha; and I will be so in all sincerity, without deceit or ill-intention, for the honour of his kingship, as by right a man ought to behave towards his lord and master. May God and the saints whose relics lie here before me grant me their help; for to this end I shall devote and consecrate myself with all the intelligence that God has given me, for the remainder of my life."

This was a grave undertaking, invested with all the additional solemnity and publicity the church could give it. Upon it the security of the Carolingian settlement precariously rested. It involved the oath-taker in complete obedience to the king's orders, in complete acquiescence in the *bannum* (i.e. the royal interpretation of justice and order), in the payment of heavy dues and in the performance of military service. In return the king, through his agents, such as counts and special inspectors (*missi dominici*), would see that justice was done and that the law of each man was rightly interpreted.

But fidelity was not all. An inner circle of the king's faithful men was bound to him by a yet closer oath, of vassalage. The *vassus* must have been rather like the early Frankish *antrustion*, a personal friend and retainer. The special condition created by the oath was that of *obsequium* or obedience, what was later to be identified as homage. Under the Carolingians there was a mystical intensity about it. The vassals of the lord king (the *vassi dominici*) might either serve in their master's court or do his work elsewhere. In either case their service might be rewarded with gifts of land, conditional or not, from newly-won or confiscated domains, as with his vassals, most of them Austrasian Franks and his kinsmen, who served Charlemagne in outlying territories as counts. In this manner the new dynasty rewarded its supporters, established their power as great landed aristocrats, used them in every possible way and bound them closer by special oaths of allegiance.[1]

Charlemagne further encouraged all free men to become not just the clients but the vassals of his magnates, stipulating that this should be done *ad nostrum utilitatem*; and so a class

[1]According to one view the tie of vassalage was at this period so close as to imply an inferior status, i.e. one that great men, such as counts, would accept individually but not as a class.

of sub-vassals was created, ready, in theory at least, to follow their lords to the king's wars but not to fight against him. A vassal with a benefice of about 400 acres of decent farmland might well be expected to serve his master as a fully armed and mounted knight. In addition to giving the king a firmer grip on his own magnates and their resources, this also moved a good deal of the burden of recruitment from the king's shoulders. "Let everyone," ordained the king in 810, "so order his subordinates that they may become increasingly obedient to and compliant with the imperial commands."

A special difficulty about this arrangement was that magnates would not, and sometimes could not, distinguish between lands they held as benefices in virtue of an office and lands that were personal, outright gifts from the sovereign. When, for example, a count died or was replaced the comital lands reverted to the crown. But his relations did not always see things in this light, and were sometimes prepared to fight in order to hold on to all their lands. Real property, like offices, showed a natural tendency to become hereditary in the Middle Ages. The Carolingians, however, were not going to commit the mistake that had impoverished their predecessors, by alienating in perpetuity the royal fisc or domain. On the contrary, Charlemagne added to his domains in every possible way and administered them with great efficiency. A famous Capitulary, *De Villis*, shows him at work as an estate-manager on a very big scale.

It may be argued that in practice Charlemagne was not very much better off than the Merovingians, for whereas they made outright gifts to their retainers he made conditional alienations which yet proved on occasion to be permanent. Indeed, the troubles of his reign were in part caused by disgruntled magnates, some of them churchmen, who thought they could brave his wrath on such issues. However, the truth seems to be that most of his vassals were not prepared to risk the consequences of rebellion. They knew the terrible vigilance of the great warrior and the vengeance he might, and did, take. Charlemagne's way of dealing with men and lands was his own. That is why it is foolish to suppose that his much-discussed administrative system could ever effectively or perma-

nently have unified the many lands he ruled. It is also why his
Empire could not survive him. The fusion of vassalage with
benefice, the creation, that is, of a lord-man relationship based
on tenure, has often been said to constitute the true customary
basis of feudal society. If this is so, then we must recognize,
not its origins but its first flowering in the lands of the Carolingians and in their repeated groping for some compromise
between the husbanding of their natural resources and the
rewarding of the churchmen and warriors to whom they
owed all.

The eight years between the revolts of 793 and the imperial
coronation have been called a period of consolidation. They
were the years when Charlemagne painfully re-imposed his
authority over Saxony (at the cost of mass-deportations) and
the Spanish March and the Middle Danube lands of the Avars.
The organization and settlement of these distant marcher-
lands seems to have impressed contemporary writers less than
did the military aspect. The great warrior carried Frankish
arms and Roman Christianity into fresh territory and came
back, like his forebears, with cartloads of treasure and convoys
of captives for distribution among his retinue. We have always
to see that the rôles of Christian champion and barbarian war-
leader, like the terms 'cleric and layman' or 'Church and
State', seemed much less mutually exclusive to contemporaries
than they do to us. Charlemagne was a pious and credulous
man. At the synod of Frankfurt in 794 he presided in person and
caused his bishops to take a strong line on certain theological
issues against the advice of the Pope. He was not prepared to
admit compromise with the supporters of the dogma of the
worship of images, though Pope Hadrian, better informed than
he about the great issue that had torn the Eastern Empire, was
so prepared. It seems likely that Charlemagne was falling
increasingly under the influence of Alcuin, and was ready to
interpret his duties as a ruler in a way pleasing to Alcuin,
especially where they impinged on Christian dogma. It is also
probable that in these years Alcuin's mind was full of ideas
about the creation (rather than revival) of a Christian Empire
in the west, and that these ideas were communicated to Charlemagne. The imperial coronation of Christmas Day, 800, is no

longer thought to have been an event quite as epoch-making as an earlier generation believed. But it was a great day in the history of the Franks, and its implications must be considered.

Charlemagne had extended the power of the Franks beyond anything achieved by his ancestors. He had subjugated Lombardy, Bavaria, Saxony and southern Gaul; he had checked the Avars; he had intervened masterfully in Byzantine and Arabic affairs; and he was *Patricius Romanorum*, the protector of Rome. He had beaten Charles Martel at his own game. It was a personal triumph. Yet all the time he knew (and the Franks knew) that one day he would divide his lands among his sons, and they would quarrel and fight like the sons of Clovis. Political integration was an ideal to the churchmen; it was an accident to the Frankish war-lords.

In the extent of his dominions Charlemagne ruled an area of Europe not unlike that once ruled by the Roman Emperors of the West. When Alcuin wrote that Charlemagne already ruled over an empire he may have had this other empire in mind, or he may have meant it in no very specialized sense. He came, after all, from York where, in the tradition of Bede, scholars used *regnum* and *imperium* as interchangeable words. So perhaps to him Charlemagne was just another *Bretwealda* (I mean, a warrior who had established his authority over other warriors, and kept it, by force of arms). However, Alcuin sometimes narrowed his meaning by writing *Christianum Imperium*: his king's authority, in so far as it was imperial, was Christian. He wished to identify the king's actual power with the Roman Christian Empire of the Liturgy.

In 788, Charlemagne and the Empress Irene of Constantinople fell out over the Lombard duchy of Beneventum in southern Italy, where Byzantine interests were still powerful. It was the first occasion on which the Empire had been able to challenge the Frankish usurpation of Italy, and the armed clash and the consequent imperial defeat made a deep impression. But the quarrel went deeper than this, for the dogma of the cult of images was also involved. Finally, in 797, Irene deposed her son, the nominal Emperor, and ruled in her own name. A woman had never before assumed imperial rank, and so men fell to speculating about its nature and uses. We can

safely say, then, that the triumph of the Empress in Constantinople had a direct bearing on Charlemagne's view of his own
position in the West.

Still more relevant was what took place in Rome. Pope
Hadrian died in 795, and Charlemagne wept as for a lost brother
or dearest friend. The next Pope, Leo III, was elected and
crowned before Charlemagne had been consulted. The Franks
became uneasy, for reports reached them that Leo's character
was not all that it might be, and that the city was disturbed.
In April, 799, Leo was attacked by a gang led by his predecessor's nephew. He escaped to Germany, badly injured.
Charlemagne was prepared to restore him, but only after a
full investigation had been made in Rome. This took place;
and when the findings were complete the king came down to
Italy to give judgement and to wring from Leo a public profession of innocence. Charlemagne was angry and in a hurry;
his northern territories were disturbed, and he had only come
to Rome because control of Rome and of the papacy was the
mainstay of his rule. So now, because he thought there was
something practical to be gained from it, Charlemagne resolved
to become Emperor; not Emperor of this or that, but Roman
Emperor. It was the one title that gave him closer control of
the Roman Church itself, though it mattered not at all to the
Franks and other barbarians, and served only to anger Byzantium, the true Empire. However, it seems possible that it only
slowly dawned on Charlemagne that his new title gave real
offence in the East.

On Christmas morning, 800, the king went in state to St.
Peter's to hear mass and to wear his crown, as an Eastern
Emperor would. Probably he also intended that the Pope
should consecrate his eldest son, Charles. The Byzantine
practice was for the patriarch to recite a prayer over the
Emperor, then to place a crown on his head and finally to
kneel before him and adore him. It was Emperor-worship, not
Emperor-making. As Charlemagne rose from prayer, the Pope
placed a crown on his head and then adored him; and he was
acclaimed *imperator et augustus* by the people of Rome. Thus,
intentionally or not, a simple crown-wearing and an imperial
acclamation had fused into a single great occasion. Charle-

magne was an Emperor, hailed in Rome. His power over Franks and Romans was gathered up in what a later pope called an act of concorporation. To a few, this appeared to be a renewal of something ancient: a *Renovatio Romani Imperii*.

One immediate effect was that Charlemagne felt in a stronger position to deal with the Pope's enemies in Rome. But when he had done this, he set off home at once. His capital was not to be Rome but Aachen (Aix-la-Chapelle), in the middle of his family estates. The Pope ought now to be able to look after himself. Meanwhile, although the new title may have impressed churchmen like Alcuin, it seemed to make no immediate difference to Charlemagne's personal power; for he ruled, precisely as before, as King of the Franks and the Lombards. That is what he continued to call himself in legal instruments, though in the end he added the imperial title to his royal titles. In brief, he was, as a recent writer has said, a Play-Emperor, though this does not mean that what had happened had no significance or importance to contemporaries or that Charlemagne had in some way failed.

The Byzantines considered the new Emperor a usurper in Rome though they could scarcely have feared that his ambitions would range further east. However, in the Adriatic lands and ports—a traditional bone of contention between East and West —there was plenty of opportunity for dispute; and by refusing to recognize his title, the Byzantines undoubtedly gave Charlemagne cause for alarm. He could not feel safe until they could be persuaded to do so. Venice, in particular, was desired by both Emperors. Since the Arabs had taken Alexandria, the Venetian fleet had been of assistance to the Eastern Empire in the central Mediterranean and its geographical position made it a natural clearing-house for long-distance Mediterranean trade. It exported slaves from the Danubian regions lately opened up by the Franks; it controlled the trade of the Lombard plain, notably in salt; and it imported luxury goods from the Levant, which made their way over the Alpine routes and along the northern rivers to great monasteries and the courts of rich men. After much fighting, Charlemagne acknowledged Byzantine suzerainty over Venice and Dalmatia in return for an annual tribute.

The remaining fourteen years of Charlemagne's life are a time of political disintegration, which must first be set in its social framework. The whole period covered by this book was one of heavy deflation, for gold was being drained from the West, prices rose steadily, consumption was always a little in excess of production. In social terms, this meant an increasing tendency for the great estates, lay and ecclesiastical, to look to their own resources and for their owners to assess their wealth in terms of land and the yield from land. The relationship to each other of those who lived thus, tended also to be expressed in terms of tenure. The small freeman ceased to matter as a fighting man whose independence must be preserved, and mattered only as an exploiter of arable or clearer of waste land— 'the old enemy of the forest', *har holtes feond*, as the Anglo-Saxons called him. The result was manorialized village life, *autarcie villageoise*. Except by inference, not much is known of that life, apart from the fact that it was infinitely various.

Rather more is known about the great estates or immunities, so characteristic of the Carolingian age. A few of their property-inventories are extant, the most famous being that of the Abbey of St. Germain-des-Près, near Paris, which was drawn up by the Abbot Irminon in the last years of Charlemagne's life. A large proportion of the facts assembled in it was the outcome of enquiries by sworn inquests of local people. They reveal a great immunity, still perhaps over 80,000 acres in extent though somewhat shrunken, with its estates scattered over Francia to ensure a balanced economy in wine, corn, etc. These estates were broken up into manors and small holdings for tenants. A similar picture of domanial life is given by other surveys, such as that of the royal fisc of Annapes, near Lille, or those of the bigger monastic properties further afield, such as Werden on the Ruhr, or Bobbio. From the seventy sections of Charlemagne's Capitulary *De Villis* the complete structure of a Carolingian fisc can be deduced; its administration, the duties of bailiffs, the collection of dues, the cultivation of the soil, the preservation of woodland and of game, and the rearing of domestic animals. Charlemagne was determined to keep the family estates in good order, though, like other great proprietors, he saw no way to prevent his tenants from encroaching on the domain. His manors were his true wealth. He lived on them, just as the Merovingians before him, moving from estate to estate as their produce and manufactures became exhausted.

This widespread domanial economy was by its nature unfavourable to long-distance trade and commerce. Historians are moving towards the view that this may have had more to do with the so-called closed economy of the early Middle Ages than the blocking of the Mediterranean trade-routes, first by the Vandals and then by Islam. The truth is that the evidence of such blockage is extremely difficult to interpret; it ought, in fact, to be used qualitatively rather than quantitatively. How can we know why certain amounts of silk or spices were available in western Europe at this time or at that? How can we be sure that the Arabs ever blocked trade? (Indeed, it has been argued that they did precisely the opposite, by putting into circulation the gold-hoards long immobilized as treasure by Byzantium.) For the time being, it is safer to concentrate on the ascertainable tendencies of the Carolingian domanial economy which could, and did, manage without much help from outside.

There were, however, important business transactions within the West that had little connection with the Mediterranean. For example, a flourishing armaments trade along the eastern marches, the salt trade along the Danube, and the exportation of certain metals and of textiles along the Rhine (this last trade, being as we have seen, in the hands of the Frisians). Finally, there was great commercial activity between Frankish lands on the one hand and England and Scandinavia on the other, in which wool, fish, furs, amber and wine were principal commodities. The Carolingians were not indifferent to trade; they would always protect merchants; their monetary reforms—notably the introduction of the silver *denarius* in place of the gold *solidus*—were with the sole object of facilitating trade; but their way of life did not turn upon it. Payments in kind were still common. Rents continued to be paid in produce or in services as well as in cash. Prices were still frequently calculated in terms of heads of cattle or horses or weapons. And even when payments in money are stipulated (as they often are), we must always satisfy ourselves that cur-

rency and not weight was intended. For gold in particular
remained primarily what it had always been: a treasure to
hoard. To live on the land as a member of a self-supporting
community was not, then, to be unaffected by what went on
outside, or to be indifferent to the benefits of trade.

This was the social background to the events of Charlemagne's last years. They were unhappy years. The old man
had lost his vigour and was content to stay at home, in or near
Aachen. Unrest followed. Only in 812 did he persuade the
Byzantines to recognize his title, though he died before the
peace-treaty could be ratified. Strictly, therefore, his imperial
title never was acknowledged outside Rome. He made two
succession settlements. The first, in 806, arranged for the
partition of his lands among his three legitimate sons according
to ancient Frankish custom. It was a moment of peril. The
younger Charles was on the point of delivering his main
assault on the Slavs in the Elbe-Saale area; Louis was pre-
occupied with the first Arab raids on his Aquitanian ports; and
Pepin of Italy was about to launch an attack on Venice. The
territories for which they were fighting could only be regarded
as their own. The Emperor would leave to each the territory
he had become identified with in peace and war. They were to
be equal and independent but ready to perform certain common
duties, such as the defence of the Roman Church, together and
in friendliness. But nothing was said of the Empire. The
imperial title was not hereditary and would die with him.

The younger Charles died in 811 and Pepin a year earlier,
thus leaving one son, Louis of Aquitaine. Apart from Italy,
which was to go to Pepin's son, Bernard, the inheritance could
now only come to Louis. So in September, 813, Charlemagne
associated his son in his unitary rule and crowned him in the
presence of his great men and made him consort in the imperial
title. There was nothing strange about this. Circumstances had
altered rapidly, and it was now safe and prudent to do what in
806 it would have been madness to attempt.

Without, therefore, having ever planned to, Charlemagne
handed on his title. But its content he could not hand on. His
Empire was his own achievement, won and kept at great cost
by his sword. The author of the *Chanson de Roland* was a

better historian than he knew when he put into the Emperor's mouth the words *'Deus' dist li Reis, 'si penuse est ma vie'*. In his prime—uncultivated, pious, opportunist and incomparably vigorous—Charlemagne had just managed to hold his conquests together. But the task was already beyond him before his powers failed, for Western Europe was the prey of enemies from the south, the east, and above all from the north, whom no man could have withstood.

CHAPTER VI

IMPERIUM CHRISTIANUM

CHARLEMAGNE'S achievement was one thing, his legacy another. His heir inherited an empty treasury, a corrupt and rebellious following, an ill-knit empire, a countryside often ruled by vendetta, famine-stricken and plague-ridden. Behind the veneer of unity and of uniformity lay a society intensely localized, incapable alike of national and imperial aspirations.

Charlemagne's unitary rule had rested on his command over men. We are at liberty, if we wish, to see this command in terms of a centralized administration. We may analyse the institutions of the Carolingian monarchy and the appointments of *missi dominici*, counts and lesser agents, and from the results we may construct a theory of government. But if we do this, we shall be all the more surprised to observe the rapid eclipse of the structure under Charlemagne's successors, and their apparent lack of concern—able and resolute though most of them were—at what was happening under their very eyes. They and their friends were far more concerned at the eclipse of an ideal, that of an *Imperium Christianum*, an empire not of Charlemagne's making. The immediate authors of this ideal empire must be sought in the circle of Louis the Pious; and the principal political theme of the ninth and tenth centuries, and so of this chapter, is the strange persistence of their ideal in the face of the dark reality of military disaster, economic decay and social change.

Louis the Pious had lived since boyhood in his southern kingdom of Aquitaine. Perhaps because his rule there was effectively curbed by Charlemagne, he seems to have been out of sympathy with his father and to have preferred to take his grandfather, Pepin III, as his model. His friends—notably Benedict of Aniane—were not his father's friends, and indeed replaced the latter at the great court of Aix after 814. They

were the children of the Carolingian renaissance, fierce reformers
for the most part, who held that the old Emperor had done
little enough to help them realize their ambitions. These were
the men who taught Louis to seek the substance of power not
in the barbarian might of a High King but in a Christian
universitas over which he should reign as Emperor. His proud
title was *divina ordinante providentia Imperator Augustus*. His
dominion was over Christians, not Franks or Romans. In
official documents he called himself *piissimus* and not, as his
father, *gloriosissimus*; while Ardo, biographer of Benedict of
Aniane, called him emperor of the universal church in Europe.
In a well-known letter on the subject of the diversity of laws,
Archbishop Agobard of Lyon begged his master to remember
that, in St. Paul's phrase, there was no longer Greek or Jew,
barbarian or Sythian, "or Aquitanian, Lombard, Burgundian,
Alaman, bond or free; for all are one in Christ".

Such was the objective of a king whose material reserves
were negligible and whose ability to command loyalty would
rest, in the last resort, upon his largesse. It should not, however,
be thought that Louis' piety and partiality for the company of
monk-reformers cut him off wholly from the life of his class.
His biographers say that he was physically powerful, a good
hunter, and a warrior when occasion demanded. For example,
he took strong measures against the Northmen for which he is
seldom given credit. That he was also temperamentally
unbalanced and liable to extremes of passion, anger and humility
seems probable; for he was never an easy man to get on with.
He made enemies more quickly than friends.

It was not long before the new Emperor found it necessary
to pay more attention to the great men of his father's day and
less to his reforming friends. He needed loyal service wherever
he could find it; and thus he fell between two stools. The result
was disillusion, which broods over all the writings of the period.
The Emperor who was to have united the Christian West had
in practice if not in theory deserted his friends, and divine
retribution was bound to follow. The disloyalty of his sons,
the raids of the Northmen and Saracens, plague, famine and
personal humiliation were all interpreted in this light. God's
judgement was upon the Franks and catastrophe was imminent.

Lethargy and hopelessness ensued and undoubtedly helped to condition political events.

The ideal of the Christian Empire is best expressed in a document known as the *Ordinatio Imperii*, of 817. In effect it was Louis' plan for the future. He did not intend to leave equal shares of his possessions to each one of his three sons. Lothaire, the eldest, was to have the imperial title[1] and the biggest share. Pepin would get the kingdom of Aquitaine, the march of Toulouse and parts of Burgundy. Louis (later called 'the German') would have Bavaria and the eastern marches; and Bernard, the Emperor's nephew, would continue to rule in Italy. All three, however, were to acknowledge their subordination to the Emperor Lothaire, to give him annual gifts, and to make no wars that he should disapprove of. Furthermore, their kingdoms were to revert to him if they died without heirs. It would be going too far to call them his viceroys, since effectively they would have been independent of him; but they were certainly expected to acknowledge in him their Christian suzerain.

But this plan, the work probably of Benedict of Aniane and of the brothers Wala and Adalard, came to nothing. In the first place Bernard of Italy considered it derogatory, revolted and was deprived both of his kingdom and of his eyes. His family was exiled to northern France, where for centuries it nursed its resentment against the heirs of Louis the Pious. Italy fell to Lothaire; and thus the close association of Emperor and Pope was resumed. In the second place, the Empress died and Louis the Pious remarried almost at once. His new wife was Judith, daughter of a Bavarian magnate and a woman of beauty and determination. The child of this marriage was Charles, known to later generations as 'the Bald'. The efforts of Judith to secure a fair share of the inheritance for her son, and of his half-brothers to prevent his getting it, resulted in a resumption of family strife in the approved Frankish manner. Once again, the West was torn by civil war. The exponents of the *Imperium Christianum*, now in ruins, naturally regarded Judith as the embodiment of evil and the special manifestation of Antichrist; and if, on the one hand, we have to look behind their virulent polemic to see the natural motives of the Bavarian

[1]In fact he assumed it forthwith, as co-emperor.

princess, we have, on the other, to admit that a great ideal had been shattered. Between the conflicting parties stood the Emperor Louis, at one moment swayed by the reformers and at the next by his wife and her supporters. His prestige, and that of his office, suffered irreparable damage, for men became accustomed to the idea of changing loyalties and realized that salvation lay in self-help. This played its part in the steady emergence of a number of great comital houses whose authority, however derived, was maintained by the sword and whose attachment to their lord the king was spasmodic in the extreme.

It must, however, be emphasized that this state of affairs was not new. What gives disloyalty and self-help a special colour in the ninth century is that we see them against the background no longer of Frankish kingship but of the Christian Empire that might have been. The magnates of Europe did not become blackguards overnight, nor was it their aim, as historians so often repeat, to destroy kingship. They intended merely to live without interference upon their own estates and to see in their king the interpreter of law and the natural leader of the nation in arms. What they did destroy, no doubt unintentionally, was the dream of the monastic reformers.

Few of these comital dynasties have been studied in any detail; but one at least, the great dynasty of St. Guilhem, may be glanced at in passing, since its history shows in an exaggerated form the difficulties and dangers that faced the landed aristocracy of the early Middle Ages.

St. Guilhem, friend, neighbour and kinsman of Charlemagne, was created duke and count of Toulouse and ruler of the great march that stretched south over the Pyrenees into future Catalonia. It was not intended that he should be interfered with by Pepin in his own principality, and he was not. His brother was Thierry, count of Autun, and his son-in-law the formidable Wala. His son, Bernard of Septimania, succeeded to much of his power, used it to support the Empress Judith and so lost all; for he was executed under the walls of Toulouse in 844. Bernard of Septimania left two sons. The elder, Guilhem, count of Bordeaux, made a bid for his father's county of Barcelona and also lost his head; while the younger,

Bernard Plantevelue, resolved to reclaim his family's possession of Autun, in the north, at the price of assassination. He also succeeded to vast possessions in Languedoc, the Toulousain, the Limousin and Berry and even to his father-in-law's county of Auvergne. In brief, he stirred memories of the ancient dukedom suppressed by Pepin, and foreshadowed the medieval dukes of Aquitaine. Within three generations, therefore, a single family had established its rule, often in the face of royal opposition, over much of the south of France. It had achieved this by remorseless pressing of family claims and by wise marriages, all within the age-old framework of vengeance and feud. There is not very much that was new in the story, except that the family in question was not native Aquitanian but northern Frankish. It had been planted in the south to undertake a particular mission; and there it had taken root, identifying itself with the south while losing none of its interest in the north; cutting throats but endowing churches;[1] ignoring and sometimes challenging the Carolingians, but never supplanting them or denying their kingship.

Louis the Pious was no more successful than others of his house in finding ways out of the dilemma of being unable to foster his domains since from them he had to reward his followers—and that with small hope of obtaining back what he granted conditionally or temporarily. While yet king in Aquitaine he had incurred his father's wrath for his over-generous alienation of the fisc, and as Emperor he made no bones about unconditional surrender of even more of it. Thegan, one of his biographers, wrote: "he was so generous . . . that he gave away to his faithful followers royal domains that had been held by himself, his father and his grandfather, and that as outright gifts (*in possessionem sempiternam*)". Unlike Charlemagne, he refused to give his vassals ecclesiastical lands; and since he was unable and perhaps unwilling to increase the lands at his disposal by conquest, he fell back inevitably upon the Merovingian practice of alienating the fisc. It is easy enough for us to see the consequences of this policy. It is less easy to suggest what else he might have done.

[1]Guilhem the Pious, son and successor of Bernard Plantevelue, was the founder of Cluny.

In his last years and during the reigns of his sons the Empire of Louis the Pious, subjected first to one and then to another scheme of division, showed increasingly clearly the component parts of which it was made. Linguistic differences tended to become more clearly marked. The vernacular of the East and West Franks, for example, had developed along very different lines towards modern German and French, as may be seen from the oaths exchanged between Charles the Bald and Louis the German at Strasbourg in February 842 and preserved by the historian Nithard in his *History of the Sons of Louis the Pious*.[1] Each king had to speak in the language of the other's followers; which was not difficult, since Charles was, through his mother, half Bavarian, whereas Louis, the seat of whose power was Bavaria, was a pure Frank. The Carolingians of the ninth century did not, however, envisage their lands as linguistic units and accordingly their attempts to divide them paid little or no attention to language. Louis the German did not consider that any such barrier precluded him from interfering in the affairs of the West Franks. It was not language that caused hostility between the East and West Franks, any more than it was the river Rhine flowing between them. Politics divided them: the creation, namely, of a third or middle kingdom between them, the rich central strip running south from Frisia through Lorraine and Burgundy to the valley of the Po.

The text of the Treaty of Verdun, whereby this threefold division was established, has not survived, though we know that it was the result of long negotiations between the warring Carolingians in the summer of 843. The new middle kingdom, the land of the Emperor Lothaire,[2] was without justification ethnically or geographically. But it would have been difficult for the boundary-commissioners to have improved on their work, given the fact that a middle kingdom was to be created. To the Carolingians themselves there was nothing strange about it. They had divided their lands in such a way that the senior had his share of the ancient Frankish heritage as well as his

---

[1]Nithard, grandson of Charlemagne and apologist of Charles the Bald, was a layman. Literacy was never confined to the clergy.
[2]Louis the Pious died in June, 840.

kingdom of Italy. It was a proper compensation for an Emperor who no longer had much hope of enforcing on his brothers the Christian unity envisaged in 817. Once again, the Frankish world was in fragments; it was regrettable, as ecclesiastical contemporaries pointed out; but it was unavoidable, and certainly not haphazard or immoral. The Carolingians had bought present peace at the cost of endless future war; for neither the East nor the West Franks ceased to covet the rich lands that lay between them and had once belonged to both, lands in which stood the Carolingian estates and Aix (or Aachen), the *palatium* of Charlemagne. The ancient hostility of France and Germany goes back no further than the Treaty of Verdun.

The *Imperium Christianum* no longer existed, the Empire of Charlemagne still less; the Frankish world was never again to know peace. And yet it was still possible for the Franks to feel that they were one. In a famous letter to the Byzantines, the Emperor Louis II, son of Lothaire, gave proud expression to this: "In answer to your comment that we do not rule over all Francia, briefly, we do indeed so rule in as much as we hold what they hold who are of one flesh and blood with us". The Byzantines, were, of course, right; but it is significant that Louis II should have defended himself in such terms. Significant also was the speed with which, not long afterwards, four Carolingian rulers who heartily disliked each other united their forces to crush a non-Carolingian usurper in Provence.

Louis the Pious was succeeded in West Francia (and ultimately as Emperor) by his youngest son, to whom he had given the name of his own father, Charles. Louis probably did not think so highly of Charlemagne as to hope that his son would one day rule over the same extent of territory and in the same manner; but the new Charles did not forget the old, for he belonged to a generation sufficiently far removed from Charlemagne to believe in a golden age that perished with the great Emperor. Almost in his own lifetime Charlemagne had become something of a myth, but by the middle of the ninth century that myth was developed and flourishing. Weary of *bella civilia*, men wished to see the old Charles in the new; and so, to some extent, they did. For example, the monastery of St. Gall wrote an account of Charlemagne for Charles the Fat—Charles the

Bald's nephew—based on the stories then current about him. The result of this attitude was an age of conscious archaism. Charlemagne was well launched upon a wonderful medieval career that was to take him through the *chansons de geste* and the *Pseudo-Turpin Chronicle* to his canonization by Barbarossa's anti-pope and to his seat among the Nine Worthies of the world, the peer of Hector, Alexander, Caesar, Joshua, David, Judas Maccabeus, Godfrey de Bouillon and King Arthur. The influence of that myth on medieval minds was deep and strange; but it is not the concern of this book.

Charles undoubtedly held what has come to be called the hegemonial view of imperial rule. He believed, in brief, that if a king ruled over more than one kingdom or people, and was so acclaimed, he was thus an emperor. The Anglo-Saxons had thought along the same lines, and had presumably exported their opinion, with many others, to Francia. This did not deprive an imperial coronation in Rome of a very special significance, but it somewhat modified its force. Thus we find Charles the Bald not always satisfied with sitting at home and ruling his inheritance; there were other peoples and other places over which a Frankish king might rule. At the end of his life he set out, with papal support, to assume the imperial title in Rome; but not with the support of his Frankish magnates, who argued that their king had no business in Italy when his homeland faced dissolution.

Charles drew on other sources than what may be called the Carolingian legend to support his throne. Lawgiving seemed to him a necessary part of the kingly office. To his reign belong many capitularies; and it is not impossible that some part of the collation and publication of barbarian law attributed to Charlemagne belongs by right to his grandson. Certainly, some of the earliest and most interesting collections preserved to us were written in the course of his long reign. A king (and much more, an emperor) was a lawgiver: that was the tradition of Rome, Byzantium, the Old Testament and the barbarians themselves.

Prominent among Charles' advisers was a certain Hincmar. He had been a monk at St. Denis, where he saw the Carolingians at close quarters and learned how intimately they identified their interests with those of the great monastery. Charles was himself their lay-abbot—that is to say, their secular protector against any who would encroach on their vast possessions or privileges. Hincmar is now commonly accepted as the author of a partly fictitious history of the abbey under Dagobert and Clovis II. Using the materials to hand in the abbey library (even then the historiographical centre of France) he aimed to prove how close were the connections of crown and abbey; and he succeeded. For thereafter, he was much used on royal business, and the see of Reims was his reward. Reims had not ceased to be important since the time of Clovis and St. Rémi. How could it have been otherwise, stretching across northern France to the sea, and standing as a barrier-principality between France and the Rhineland? Hincmar increased its importance through his interest in the process of king-making, from which sprang the association of Reims and the crown in the rites of coronation and unction, and also a large part of the ceremonial order itself. In 869 Hincmar composed a special coronation *ordo* for Charles on the occasion of his coronation at Metz as king of the Middle Kingdom.[1] In this way a complex ritual was gradually built on the foundations laid by Hincmar and his contemporaries. King-making called for ceremonial vestments and weapons and books, notably Bibles and sacramentaries; and some of these, splendidly embellished, survive from the early Middle Ages to prove that the descriptions of them by contemporary writers are not very far from the truth. Charles was a magnificent king, a new Constantine, a new Solomon, a new Theodosius, surrounded with every circumstance of pomp, a magnet to a host of artistic impulses, first among them, perhaps, those from Byzantium. The Carolingians delighted to ape the Greeks, who, after all, were their near neighbours in Italy. Many Carolingian illuminations of the ninth century demonstrate the closeness of this dependence on Byzantine models; the church of Metz, where Charles was consecrated, prided itself, like Rome, on its Greek School,

---

[1]Hincmar took the opportunity to remind Charles that he was of the race of Clovis, who was anointed and consecrated king, and that his real power derived from his consecration at the hands of bishops. He was *Christus Domini*.

and in fact translated into Greek its version of the *Laudes Regiae*, the triumphal litany in which the western church acclaimed Christ the Conqueror and with Him His earthly vicars—emperors, kings and prelates—associating them with their counterparts in the heavenly hierarchy. Yet once again men's aspirations flowed naturally into the mould of St. Augustine's *City of God*.

But Hincmar had still other claims on the gratitude of his master.[1] He assumed the leadership of the West Frankish clergy and kept them loyal to Charles in a time when loyalties were wavering. Many great men were uncertain whether one Carolingian might not be as good a lord as the next; whether, in fact, they should not desert Charles for his brother Louis the German, whose appetite for the Middle Kingdom and even West Francia was insatiable. Hincmar kept the clergy loyal. He would stand no interference from Louis and very little from Pope Nicholas I—the first pope since Gregory the Great to assert fearlessly the right of Rome to interpret political morality. Moreover, in his old age he wrote an important treatise for Charles' little grandson, his *De Ordine Palatii*. It was a résumé, probably inaccurate, of the way in which he believed Charlemagne had managed the business of government. Always men's eyes turned back to him, and especially Hincmar's, to whom the evils of the present time seemed attributable to the Carolingians' escape from ecclesiastical control. Hincmar did not really know how Charlemagne ordered his affairs but he liked to pretend that it had been strictly in accordance with the divine will and that a hierarchy of palace officials had existed solely to spare him from worldly problems for the contemplation of the divine. And so, assuming the mantle of a new Ezekiel, Hincmar spoke for the last time.

A long section of the annals written at Reims, and later known as the Annals of St. Bertin, was from the pen of Hincmar. More than anything else, this section established the claim of the Church of Reims as one of the great historiographical schools of the West, whose future writers were to include men

---

[1] I leave quite out of account Hincmar's great distinction as canonist (i.e. authority on the Law of the Church) and theologian. He took a leading part in the theological controversy of his generation.

as distinguished, in their various ways, as Flodoard, Richer and Gerbert. Hincmar's is the third section of the Reims annals, covering the years 861 to 882. The earlier sections are terse and impartial, but Hincmar, a statesman of violent feelings and with interests everywhere, brings life to the work. Further, he was much better informed than his predecessors, and made full use of the wide ramifications of his Church's possessions all over Francia. Yet, if the annals gain in fullness and colour, they lose in impartiality. Hincmar wrote as a man passionately concerned to champion his Church of Reims and, more critically, his master, the West Frankish king.

What Reims did for the west, Fulda did for the east. The favourite home of St. Boniface had never lost contact with the Carolingians; and when a branch of the dynasty settled east of the Rhine it was Fulda that told their story in annalistic form. Again, as with Reims, these annals are the record not of a new people suddenly self-conscious, but of a powerful religious community whose interests and sources of information were roughly coterminous with the extent of its possessions. Naturally, Fulda knew more and cared more about Louis the German than about Charles the Bald, although, on the other hand, it was able to provide Charles the Bald with a tutor, Walahfrid Strabo. By collating the two sets of annals, historians can sometimes obtain a stereoscopic view of real value. It was not mere antiquarianism, however, that caused the Fulda monks to keep their record. Their fortune was linked with that of the dynasty under whose shadow they had grown up and increased their lands and wealth. Until well into the ninth century Fulda was the only German monastery to enjoy complete exemption from diocesan control (in this case, from Mainz); and this favoured position depended on the continued goodwill of the Carolingians. A great immunist was always suspect. Naturally, therefore, the monks did what they could to cultivate the dynasty. Their reward was a string of much-prized charters of donation, corroboration or exemption; and where these failed it was necessary, as elsewhere (notably at St. Denis), to resort to forgery. Fulda forged a privilege from Charlemagne and presented it to his successors to confirm. In the detection of forged charters the modern expert in diplomatic or paleography is far more skilled than the medieval chancery clerk.

The literary interests of Fulda were not, of course, confined to this. The libraries of the great German churches and monasteries, such as Lorsch, Cologne, Würzburg, Reichenau and St. Gall, have preserved to us much of what we have of classical literature; and Fulda was the greatest of these. To it we owe vital texts of Tacitus, Suetonius, Ammianus, Vitruvius and Servius (through whom medieval men learnt their Virgil). Perhaps its brightest light in the ninth century was the abbot Raban Maur—'the Raven', to whom Alcuin gave the name of St. Benedict's pupil, Maurus—who ended his life Archbishop of Mainz. Raban was a favourite pupil of Alcuin and himself the master of distinguished scholars. So the tradition of Bede and the School of York passed on from mind to mind. It was a tradition that scorned originality and sought only to conserve and to disseminate what was good. Raban was content, then, to spend his mighty talents at the work of exposition and collation. He was haunted by the image of a dissolving civilization. There was no security anywhere. What he could collect, he collected, and the result was *De Universo*, an encyclopaedia of received knowledge founded on the labours of Isidore of Seville. But he was a theologian as well as an encyclopaedist, and a man of letters as well as a theologian. His curiosity about language is instanced in his love of runes and cyphers, his copying down of the sixteen-letter alphabet of the Viking Age (preserved in a ninth-century St. Gall manuscript), and his little treatise *De Inventione Linguarum* (or *Litterarum*) which may be said to stand, not too humbly, in the much-neglected series of medieval writings on language and letters of which Dante's *De Vulgari Eloquentia* is the flower. A man's vernacular calls, perhaps, for some explanation, says Raban. But then, the Lord feeds the ravens as well as the doves.

Raban handed on his fidelity to the tradition of Bede to his pupils, at least four of whom were honoured in their day, at Fulda and further afield. The most distinguished of them was Servatus Lupus, abbot of Ferrières, and probably the nearest approach to the modern idea of a scholar that the Middle Ages can show, earlier than John of Salisbury. He was a humanist, a collector and collater of classical texts;[1] but, like many medieval scholars, so much else besides. He was able, for example, to revise Raban's commentary on the Book of Numbers, to compile and illustrate a corpus of barbarian laws for the Duke of Friuli, to compose Saints' Lives, to write the best letters of his generation, to rule his own monastery with a rod of iron, ceaselessly fighting for its privileges against usurpers, and to take a full part in public life at the West Frankish court, at its assemblies and synods, and even on the field of battle; for he personally led the Ferrières contingent to the army in 844 and was taken prisoner, being as he says, a poor soldier. But it was as much as an abbot's or a bishop's life was worth not to lead his contingent to the host when required by the king. This sort of life was what made it impossible for contemporaries to think of clergy and laity as distinct bodies. Theirs was a very small world.

The social and political processes of localization or disintegration that have been touched upon were greatly accelerated by the threefold pressure from the north, the south and the east to which Europe was subjected in the ninth and tenth centuries. These attacks were sometimes concerted; and the heightened sense that they must have been, caused some, particularly in the Roman Curia, to see Europe as a beleaguered garrison whose only hope lay in unity. But the truth is that most people did not see the situation in this light and thought that European unity was an over-rated ideal, like that of its parent, the *Imperium Christianum*.

The attacks from Scandinavia have never been adequately explained. Land-hunger, growing population,[2] discontent at the mounting authority of their kings, and a natural love of plunder and adventure have all been advanced as reasons for the comparatively sudden, but sustained, incursion of the Northmen into European waters. The Swedes took the Baltic route, from which they penetrated in their longboats up the German and

---

[1]He writes, for example, to Ansbald: "I will collate your text of Cicero's Letters with my own, so that from the two texts the truth may, if possible, emerge."

[2]The Scandinavians practised polygamy and were as slow to abandon it as were most other barbarians. The church was still fighting Frankish polygamy in the ninth century.

Russian rivers. From their trading-post at Kiev they were within reach of Byzantium itself. The Norwegians raided in a great arc round Scotland and Ireland to the Faroés, Iceland and beyond. The Danes divided their attention between Anglo-Saxon England and the continent (Frisia, Francia, Spain and the western Mediterranean).

As the armies and missions of the early Carolingians moved north into Frisia, contact with the Danish world beyond was a matter of course. It was not possible to control Frisian trade and to convert Frisian souls without making the Danes aware that a no-man's land was rapidly becoming a marcher land. When Charlemagne finally conquered the Saxons, the neighbours of the Frisians, a still more positive danger presented itself. Where was the advance of Frankish arms and Frankish Christianity to end? One great missionary, St. Anskar of Corbie (whose *Life* by his successor Rimbert is an important source for the ninth century) established the see of Hamburg-Bremen and from it penetrated into Sweden. More immediately, the Carolingians seem to have curbed Frisian sea-power, so that when the Danes moved south they found that they were masters in Frankish and Frisian waters without having to fight for supremacy. It is extraordinary that having discovered that there was no opposition at sea from Franks or Anglo-Saxons, the Danes took as long as they did to make their power seriously felt.

This is not to say that the Franks were unaware of the danger that faced them. Both Charlemagne and Louis the Pious did what they could to organize coastal defences at the river-mouths and at the approaches to harbours. But the coastline was tremendous and the longships could always find a beach or inlet. A second method of defence was to stir up trouble amongst the Danish chieftains; and at this Louis was particularly successful, as the Frankish annals bear witness. The real storm broke in the years following Louis' death. It was then that great armies landed, established themselves for long periods and organized raiding-parties far into the interior of Europe. They wanted booty and plunder and found it in th e monasteries of the Carolingian renaissance; and if it was possible to over-paint the picture of desolation that ensued it would not be surprising if the monastic *scriptoria* took liberties in that direction. The pagan Vikings were often prepared to demand what they required and then move on; but if the communities opposed or deceived them, sacking and burning would follow. The impetus of the attacks seems to have been partly spent by the end of the ninth century, the raids on the whole becoming smaller. It was not, it has been argued, in the interests of a strong Danish monarchy that chieftains should rove at will in search of treasure, only to return and disrupt allegiance. However, with the ultimate breakdown of the monarchy, the Vikings persisted in their ventures, though they showed a tendency to become rather venturers in search of land for settlement than tip-and-run raiders.

It is probable that the desire for land to settle was never wholly absent. As one historian puts it, they were folk soberly addressing themselves to the task of winning land abroad. Louis the Pious, for example, gave lands in the north to dissident Danes. They lacked the capacity to administer and to organize states but they were intelligent business men and good farmers. A settlement was quite soon cemented by inter-marriage, conversion and trading relations. In Ireland, the Scandinavian marauders were accepted comparatively quickly as part of the community and were equally successful as inland farmers and as traders and fishermen. In the northern Frankish river-settlements they seem to have had more permanent interests than mere plundering. Their participation in the northern Frankish wine trade, for example, was not confined to seizing wine for their own consumption, much though they loved carousing. They were also capable of controlling the traffic down the rivers to the ports whence wine was shipped abroad (e.g. to England), and of making a good profit out of dues. It may not be going too far to say that this adaptability and capacity to make the best of two worlds was what led certain of the Franks to make terms with the new-comers; for they could, on occasion, be good lords, and it would have been folly not to have accepted favourable terms when they were offered. Once again, the extreme localization of Frankish society, and hence of its interests, made it unthinkable that every threatened landlord should place national or even royal interests before his own. He lacked the means to resist the

Vikings, unless against brief raids, and he knew that help from above could never reach him in time. So he gathered his men about him and joined with his neighbours to defend his estates as well as he could, and compromised with the enemy when he could not. His first loyalty was to his own neighbourhood; and this never wavered.[1]

The Carolingians were also lords of considerable estates, from which an important part of their revenues was derived. These estates were endangered, along with those of other men, and thus it is not surprising that the royal dynasty reacted to the general threat in much the same way as did the lesser dynasties. Almost without exception, the later Carolingians were ready to take the field when they could against the Vikings. Louis the Pious, Charles the Bald and Louis III (879–882, victor of the battle of Saucourt) are examples. Charles the Fat is usually considered a disastrous exception, since he failed to raise the Viking siege of Paris and died a broken man, deposed by his East German followers. However, his failure came at the very end of his life and may well have been a failure of health and not of courage. Charles the Simple, who in 911 agreed with the Danish chieftain Rollo to surrender a large area of land (the nucleus of modern Normandy) for permanent settlement on certain terms, acted in no craven spirit. He was a warrior of distinction, but he saw that where he lacked the means to eject it would be wiser to welcome.[2]

The Carolingians fought the Vikings when they could. But there was no real defence against incessant attack in force from the sea. A national host, such as was raised from time to time, could meet a major threat. The victories of Alfred's fyrd in England have their counterpart in Francia; indeed, the Frankish and English kings saw clearly that the Danish threat was common to both sides of the Channel and learned something from each other about defence methods as well as about the best means to keep their subjects loyal. But when the threat was not concentrated, there was little that kings could do. The

[1] A good example of this is provided in the St. Bertin Annals for 859, when many living in the Seine-Loire region banded together in self-defence but were massacred for their trouble.

[2] The agreement did not prevent the Danes in Normandy from behaving like pirates long after 911.

burden of defence and the choice between battle or capitulation then lay with the men on the spot. Some, like the Robertinian dynasty in the north—one day to become the Capetians—fought like true marcher lords. Others did not. At other times there was nothing to do but to buy off the attackers with tribute. The reactions of the Franks to the Vikings are, then, rather complicated. The Carolingians did not consider themselves the natural saviours of every part of Francia, whenever invaded; the magnates did not consider that the only claim on their loyalty was to fight the Vikings to the last ditch; the paying of tribute was not always a sign of hopeless capitulation; and all men, kings included, were prepared at times to indulge their own vendettas rather than to unite against the common enemy. Is it for us to condemn them for seeing the outcome less clearly than we do, and for failing to live up to the ideal set before them by the Church?

The attack on Europe from the Mediterranean was delivered by the *Sarraceni*, by which name contemporaries knew the Arabs, the Berbers and the Moors, the conquerors of Egypt, Roman Africa and Spain. The Carolingians had pushed them south of the Pyrenees and had set up a great marcher-principality to defend the southern approaches to Francia. But after Charlemagne's death the danger was not from Spain. It was from the emirate of Tunisia, which sent out expeditions to raid the coastline of Provence and Italy. A long and bitter campaign reduced Byzantine Sicily (Taormina held out till 902) and southern Italy was open to invasion. The hero of the Frankish resistance was the Emperor Louis II, son of Lothaire. He spent most of his life fighting the Saracens in Italy, sometimes with Byzantine help. But, as in northern waters, the coastline was too long for defence against a sea power that could strike anywhere and which could, moreover, count on local defections. So much depended on local will to resist.

Naples, Gaeta and Amalfi organized a common defence that proved successful, while Rome was less fortunate. But before his death in 875, Louis II had ensured that Italy was not to become a second Saracen province like Spain. Saracen influence and Saracen communities remained an important factor in the life of Italy; but they did not predominate.

Saracen raiding along the coast of Provence, and far inland, was a matter of which Louis the Pious had had to take notice while still king of Aquitaine. The most notorious Saracen stronghold was at Fraxinetum (now St. Tropez). Generations of raiders set out from here to plunder monasteries and waylay travellers. Only when they succeeded in capturing and holding to ransom the great abbot of Cluny, St. Magilo, was sufficient resentment stirred up to lead to their extirpation. It is difficult to assess the lasting effects of such ventures. On the one hand some historians have gone too far in crediting the Saracens with constructive genius (e.g. the irrigation of the Briançonnais), while on the other there have been those who interpret too literally the monastic tales of destruction and bloodshed. Like the Danes, the Saracens were probably not deliberately destructive on a large scale, nor were they always unwelcome. There were cases of southern magnates or communities inviting Saracen participation in their vendettas. Furthermore, if the Saracens deflected and endangered long-distance Mediterranean trade (and this is not easy to substantiate in detail) they also broke down somewhat the closed economy of the Frankish world by their purchases of northern goods, such as slaves, furs, metals, arms and wood. For these the Saracens paid in gold; and this gold, in its turn, was used to finance European trade with Byzantium. It would be going too far to state that Saracen gold financed the Carolingian and Ottonian renaissances, but it may have invigorated the economy of the north. For the first time the Orient, the Mediterranean and the North were linked and sustained by a single monetary system; and this lasted just so long as the Islamic hegemony lasted, that is, to the eleventh century.

The third body of invaders, Slavs and Hungarians, approached the West, not by sea but overland, from the plains of eastern and central Europe. Charles, the eldest son of Charlemagne, spent his life campaigning against them in what is now central Germany, and in due course Louis the German succeeded to the task. The Slavs, however, must be distinguished from the Hungarians, or Magyars. Their principalities extended the whole length of the Germanic eastern march. Sometimes they pressed forward into German territory, but more often the Germans would press forward into Slav territory, extorting heavy tributes, seizing slaves,[1] making settlements of their own and imposing Christianity through a succession of marcher missionary-sees which had to compete for Slav souls, especially in the kingdom of Moravia, with the missionary zeal of Byzantium. This last was only one of the ways in which Byzantine influence was felt throughout the West during this period. Scholars are coming increasingly to recognize that loyalty to East Rome never died out in the western Mediterranean, and that not only her cultural but her political influence counted for much. A western reconquest after the fashion of Justinian must at times have seemed imminent, and particularly in the days of Byzantine-Frankish co-operation against Islam in Italy. The religious differences between East and West were not profound and were never considered insurmountable.

The balance between Germans and Slavs was violently thrown out by the arrival of the Hungarian horsemen. Turco-Mongols—and thus related to the Huns and Avars—the Hungarians had made the crossing of Europe in sixty years. Contemporaries recalled the hordes of Attila as these new invaders sacked the West at will. Italy and Francia as well as Germany were terrorized. Now, as with the Danes and Saracens, it is possible to overstate the effect of these raids. But the Hungarians were probably the most savage of the three, and were certainly the most feared by the victims. At the very least, they left behind them under-populated and thus unculti-vated lands. Consequently, their eclipse, when it came, seemed all the more a deliverance.

The East-Carolingian dynasty was no more convinced than the West-Carolingians that it had a duty to defend all Christian Europe; but increasing pressure from the east made it necessary for them to set up a series of military commands that could protect limited territory without further royal intervention. One of these was the *ducatus* of eastern Saxony; and the command was given to the family of the Liudolfings (later, the

---

[1] By the end of the ninth century the *servus* had become the *serf*, a semi-free cultivator whose duties to his lord were limited; while the classical concept of the *servus* was represented only by the *slave*, the captive from the eastern marches sold in the west, especially in infidel Spain, for domestic duties and for concubinage.

Ottonians). However much of a revocable appointment this
may originally have been, the family soon identified itself with
local interests and defended Saxony for other reasons than
loyalty to the Frankish crown. It has been maintained that
separatist interests might never have developed in Saxony and
the other German duchies if the Carolingian house had not
come to an end in 911. But such a view may overstate the extent
of Carolingian authority east of the Rhine and pay too little
heed to the tribal traditions of Swabia, Bavaria, Franconia and
Saxony. Even if we allow the dukes to be officials, they still
ruled over territories that bore some relation to ancient tribal
divisions, which the Church had done little to break down.
The unification of Germany was not an inevitable process,
nor was it delayed by dynastic misfortunes alone.

The Saxon dynasty, which in 919 succeeded to the East-
Carolingians, made Franconia the centre of its power. To
become king east of the Rhine was to become a Frank. Only
thus could the new dynasty secure the help of the German
churches, where the memory of Charlemagne as protector and
benefactor was perpetuated. The Saxons (or Ottonians) were
always conscious that they were the heirs of Charlemagne,
and their official documents reflect their efforts to look as much
like Carolingians as they could, and that particularly when
pursuing their ambitions in the old Carolingian Middle Kingdom. The complicated ritual of kingship was irretrievably
Carolingian. But the Ottonians were much more than a pale
reflection of their predecessors. They saved the West from the
Hungarians.

The history of this feat of arms is best told in the writings
of Widukind, a monk of Corvei, the German daughter-house
of the Frankish Corbie. Widukind's book may for convenience
be called the *Res Gestae Saxoniae*. It is the proud record of a
Saxon whose people had found greatness in little more than a
century. From being the implacable enemies of Charlemagne
and Christendom they had become the saviours of the Franks,
and indirectly of Rome. Widukind was a subtle as well as a
forceful writer. He was well schooled in the historical work of
Antiquity and knew how to make the best of his story. He
could, moreover, draw upon some very interesting material.

This included the heroic epics and sagas that were the stock-in-trade of the German bards, the singers and story-tellers who were welcomed in any warrior's hall, like that Bernlef who, according to the *Vita Liudgeri*, was much loved because he was a good talker and skilful in reciting the deeds of old times and the battles of kings, which he sang to his harp courteously (*non inurbane*). The result is a history that may be placed in the select company of Bede, Jordanes, Isidore and Gregory of Tours; for the *Res Gestae* is the story of the absorption of yet one more barbarian people into the West and of its rise to power within the West. Again, the author is a Christian and a professed monk; but his love is for his race—a race of noble warriors, the *principes Saxoniae*, and most noble among them their royal house. Widukind is the historian of a people and not exclusively of a dynasty.

The Ottonians, as we see them in the *Res Gestae*, are the leaders of a warrior race against the eastern hordes. First Henry the Fowler, and then Otto I with his great victory at the Lechfeld, established their claim to be something more than kings. They were warriors who ruled by force of arms over many peoples. They were *Bretwealdas*, Emperors, or whatever other title expressed supremacy. They dominated not only Germans but also easterners, Hungarians and Slavs. We know that Otto I's ambition reached over the whole Slav world; with papal support his metropolis of Madgeburg was to do for central Europe what Mainz and Fulda had done for Carolingian Germany. Even the Kievan Russians saw in him a promising counter-balance to the Byzantines and asked him to send them a bishop. Slavonia was thus no barrier to intercourse, political and commercial, between Kiev and western Europe.

Perhaps as an afterthought, Widukind dedicated his Saxon history to Matilda, daughter of Otto I. She was abbess of Quedlinburg, in the Harz mountains, the seat of Ottonian power. But it does not follow that the author was intimately connected with the dynasty or that his history was in any sense official. The Ottonians too, were Saxons, but they were much else besides. They had won renown as defenders of the eastern march, but they were kings of the Franks and so were involved, whether they liked it or not, in the politics of southern Europe. The traditional interests of the southern duchies (Swabia and Bavaria) in Lombardy drew the Ottonians into Italian politics, and so to Rome. For the wealth of the central strip (Lorraine and Burgundy) they were ready to do battle with the Western Franks and even to appoint one of the ablest members of the dynasty, Archbishop Bruno, to Cologne, a see from which he could supervise the Lorrainers. The Ottonians were masters of the West and the lords of Rome. There they were acknowledged Roman Emperors by the populace and consecrated by popes of their own choosing;[1] and there they were involved in the civilization of Byzantium, whose outpost Italy still was. Otto III, son of one Byzantine princess and would-be husband of another, showed in his precocious reign that the barbarians had retained their capacity for happy surrender to whatever was Roman. To condemn him for betraying Germany's true interests and to view the Ottonian preoccupation with Rome and Italy as monstrous diversions is a waste of time, for he neither lived long enough to make possible a true appraisal of his policy, nor while he did live did he seem to sacrifice German interests to Italian. Given the opportunity, Germans would move into the Roman orbit, from the lesser to the greater civilization. We cannot define satisfactorily what the Ottonians understood by their Roman title; but we may be sure that they accepted it as an enhancement of their German title. Their empire was not the continuation of the *Imperium Christianum* of Louis the Pious; early medieval empires were personal possessions that could never be inherited; but the words that they used to express their power were old words, full of meaning. Otto set on his seal the words *Renovatio imperii Romanorum*. This was no idle dream; he and his advisers were hard-headed men. They signified by it their intention not just to restore good order and government in their feud-ridden world but to do so according to a definite precedent. Their view of history may have been at fault, but contemporaries did not in conse-

[1]Otto III's tutor, a brilliant Frank named Gerbert of Aurillac, was successively Archbishop of Reims and of Ravenna and finally Pope as Silvester II. Popes chose (and choose) their names to signify special regard for the career of a predecessor. In this case, Gerbert's mind turned to the Pope who had been the recipient of the so-called Donation of Constantine.

quence think the phrase meaningless. It is not impossible that, had he lived, Otto would have restored the legislative function to the imperial title; for Rome was the home of law, civil and canon. His early death postponed the process. He had no time to give further proof of what it was that he hoped to restore, and why, though a Saxon, he longed to link himself to the Roman tradition.

This rapid survey of western Europe at grips with her last barbarian invaders may enable us to reach some tentative conclusions about the ways in which she had developed since the dissolution of the post-classical Empire.

In the first place, the process of social fragmentation that had been so marked a feature of the Late Empire had been accelerated. Men tended increasingly to organize their lives on a local basis; to band together for protection and to seek as lord the local magnate who could mobilize them in self-defence and do justice between them; to feed and clothe themselves from their own land; and to see their relationship to their protector and benefactor in terms of a contract, based on tenure of land, that might be renewed from generation to generation. What historians call feudal society was born in this way, though, in fact, its variations are so infinite as to rob the term of meaning. The Roman proprietor farming his villa in the fourth century would have found many points of contact with the manorial lord farming the same land in the tenth century— more, perhaps, than the same manorial lord would have found with a contemporary at the other end of Europe. Another way of expressing this change is to say that the old barbarian bond of kinship had given place to the bond of lordship, though here again one is faced with sufficient exceptions to make one question the validity of the dictum.

Secondly, the states of medieval Europe had emerged. There was no longer any doubt that, despite Empire and Papacy, France, Germany, Italy, Spain, Scandinavia and England were going their own ways, speaking their own languages and interpreting the past in different senses. It did not follow that they invariably expected to be ruled by native dynasties; for a crown, like any other possession, might be left to or claimed by a distant collateral. Kingship had lost some of its

ancient prestige, for neither barbarian war-leadership nor
Roman lawgiving was the main occupation of the tenth-century
king. His duty was to defend the complex of lands and rights
that comprised his direct possession outside the vast territorial
immunities of his kingdom, and to hand these on unimpaired
to his successor. Political horizons had shortened, though no
one supposed that kings could be dispensed with. No untruth
is blacker than that which represents early medieval kingship
and aristocracy as two fundamentally opposed forces. Tenth-
century kingship was not so much weakened as circumscribed.
Medieval men had no use for weakness and certainly never
sought it in their kings.

What, then, was left of kingship? We can form a rough
idea by examining the fate of the West-Frankish monarchy
after the accidental death in 987 of Louis V. He was a young
man and left no heir. The nearest Carolingian was his uncle,
Charles of Lorraine, a man whose claim received little support
among the Franks, who disliked him; and furthermore, the
Ottonians, with an eye to Lotharingian loyalties, were anxious
to see the end of the vigorous West-Carolingian line.

The new king was Hugh Capet, the strongest of the northern
magnates. His family had already at brief intervals worn the
crown and he had the support of the Church (notably of Reims).
But his material power was weak indeed, his magnates virtually
independent and his chance of furthering Carolingian ambitions
in Lorraine very small. Yet he was a king, and a desired king.
He was the supreme suzerain of his great men; they were his
vassals, and were bound to him by an oath that none of them
cared to break. The historian Richer preserves the solemn
oath of fealty sworn to the king in 989 by Archbishop Arnulf
of Reims. Furthermore, he was the Anointed of the Lord, one
who was neither layman nor priest but between and above the
two. He was far more literally Head of the Church in France
than ever Henry VIII was in England, for Church and State
were one and the same body. His court, the *curia regis*, was the
heart of his realm. Here he would do justice between his great
men (they could get it nowhere else) and here honour and
preferment might be had. If it is asked how far this respect for
the crown penetrated below the magnates who were the king's

kinsmen and familiars, no direct answer can be given; for there is no evidence. But at least it is clear that the traditions of Carolingian kingship were kept alive among small religious communities all over France and from them disseminated through neighbouring baronial courts in the form of epic songs and stories. This is the social background to the *Chanson de Roland*, the mighty epic of the eleventh century which shows us Capetian kings and magnates aping the Carolingians. In other words, the early Capetians had succeeded in persuading their subjects that their succession had been no act of violence; they were not a new dynasty but a continuation of something older.[1] Hugh Capet, therefore, was no failure and no weakling. His *curia* was the court of his realm; the year of his accession dated the public and private instruments of his subjects; he received but did not give oaths of fealty; he was the lord of the national church (though not of all the churches that comprised it); and he could hold his own against the Ottonians, indebted though he was to them. The administrative unification and centralization of France was not his aim. He stands, with his contemporaries, nearer to Charlemagne than to Philip Augustus.

It is not unreasonable for us to think of the tenth century as a time of rapid social and political transition. Contemporaries did not see it in that way, though many of them did think that an epoch was drawing to its close. What to us is a problem of transition was to them the problem of the imminent end of the world and the coming of Antichrist. Pessimism and even hopelessness had lasted since the failure of the *Imperium Christianum*; they are in many writings and are not necessarily connected with the mystical year 1000. The new churches that were springing up everywhere and the vigorous reforming activity of great monastic centres like Cluny did not seem to the actors to announce a new age. The apocalyptic outlook of Gregory the Great was not dead. How could it have been, in a society still dominated by vendetta? Men looked back for comfort to a heroic past that still made sense; for it was not

---

[1]Adso of Montiérender, in a dedication to the queen of Louis IV (936 to 954) wrote: "Roman rule is largely destroyed, but while there are Frankish kings who can exercise authority like Romans, the dignity of the Roman Empire will never quite perish but will live on with them".

far away, and the migrations were still not quite finished. True medieval society is unimaginable without the last great Norman outburst, to England and into the Mediterranean, in the eleventh century. Historical interests and imaginative background do not radically change in Western Europe during the period covered in this essay. That is why it has unity.

Hence, as at the beginning so at the end, the vivid contrast stands; early medieval men could live like barbarians; but they could think that they were Romans.

SELECT BIBLIOGRAPHY

GENERAL

THE two great books covering the period are Edward Gibbon, *The History of the Decline and Fall of the Roman Empire*, edited by J. B. Bury, 7 vols., London 1909; and James Bryce, *The Holy Roman Empire*, London 1906. Like most classics, both have generated much controversy. Shorter and more recent surveys are: H. St. L. B. Moss, *The Birth of the Middle Ages*, 395–814, Oxford 1935 (excellently compressed and impartial in approach); Christopher Dawson, *The Making of Europe*, London 1932; C. Delisle Burns, *The First Europe*, London 1947 (full of errors but fresh and arresting in approach); and F. Lot, C. Pfister and F. L. Ganshof, *Les Destinées de l'Empire en Occident, de 395 à 888*, 2nd ed. 2 vols., Paris 1940 (a brilliant epitome). Further background may be obtained from chapters in *The Cambridge Ancient History*, vol. XII, 1939, and *The Cambridge Medieval History*, vols. I (1924) and II (1936), and from A. Fliche and V. Martin, *Histoire de l'Église*, vols. III to VII inclusive (vols. by different authors).

SPECIAL STUDIES

(1) Literary and Artistic

H. M. Chadwick, *The Heroic Age*, Cambridge 1912; W. P. Ker, *The Dark Ages*, Edinburgh 1923, W. Levison, *England and the Continent in the Eighth Century*, Oxford 1946 and P. Vinogradoff, *Roman Law in Medieval Europe*, revised by F. de Zulueta, Oxford 1929, are the work of great scholars. Also valuable are E. K. Rand, *Founders of the Middle Ages*, Harvard 1928; M. L. W. Laistner, *Thought and Letters in Western Europe* A.D. 500 to 900, London 1931; C. N. Cochrane, *Christianity and Classical Culture*, Oxford 1940; R. Hinks, *Carolingian Art*, London 1935; P. Courcelle, *Histoire Littéraire des Grandes Invasions Germaniques*, Paris 1948; and E. S. Duckett, *Alcuin, Friend of Charlemagne*, New York 1951.

(2) *Economic and Social*

The Cambridge Economic History, vol. I, 1942, covers agrarian life; vol. 2, 1952, is concerned with trade and industry. A. Dopsch, *The Economic and Social Foundations of European Civilization*, London 1937, is important, but over-stresses continuity from imperial to barbarian life; H. Pirenne, *Mohammed and Charlemagne*, London 1939, argues rather too forcibly that Carolingian society developed on different lines from Merovingian society because cut off from the Mediterranean by the Arabs. Marc Bloch, *La Société Féodale*, 2 vols. Paris 1939, is the most important recent statement on the emergence of medieval society. F. W. Walbank, *The Decline of the Roman Empire in the West*, London 1946, is lucid and helpful though it draws conclusions that all will not accept.

(3) *Political*

F. Lot, *La Fin du Monde Antique et le Début du Moyen Age*, revised ed., Paris 1951, is a brilliant introduction; A. H. M. Jones, *Constantine and the Conversion of Europe*, London 1948, is learned and level-headed; G. Barraclough, *The Origins of Modern Germany*, 2nd ed., Oxford 1947, is a vigorous presentation of the results of recent German research; T. Hodgkin, *Italy and her Invaders*, 2nd ed., Oxford 1892, is still the only big study in English on early medieval Italy; F. M. Stenton, *Anglo-Saxon England*, 2nd ed., Oxford 1947, treats the Anglo-Saxons as part of Europe; E. Salin, *La Civilisation Mérovingienne*, vol. I, Paris 1950, is an indispensable treatment of the Merovingians, with special emphasis on archaeological evidence; L. Halphen, *Charlemagne et l'Empire Carolingien*, Paris 1947, is the best book in any language on the Carolingians; J. Calmette, *L'Effrondrement d'un Empire et la Naissance d'une Europe*, Paris 1941, is one of the very few studies of the end of the period; J. B. Trend, *The Civilization of Spain*, Oxford 1944, devotes a few excellent pages in a short survey to this period and provides a bibliography; F. Dvornik, *The Making of Central and Eastern Europe*, London 1949, is essential for an understanding of Slav links with the West; G. Turville-Petre, *The Heroic Age of Scandinavia*, London

1951, is the only book of its kind; T. D. Kendrick, *A History of the Vikings*, London 1930, is a useful introduction by a scholar who is primarily an archaeologist; and on the interaction of Latin and Byzantine thought nothing could better the two lectures of N. H. Baynes, *The Hellenistic Civilization and East Rome*, Oxford 1946, and *The Thought World of East Rome*, Oxford 1947.

SOME FURTHER READING (revised 1961)

M. Deanesly, *A History of Early Medieval Europe*, 476 *to* 911, London 1957, is a really good textbook; E. R. Curtius, *European Literature and the Latin Middle Ages*, London 1952, is an exciting survey; E. Stein, *Histoire du Bas-Empire*, vol. 2 (476–565), Paris 1949, is invaluable on Justinian; and P. Riché, *Les Invasions Barbares*, Paris 1953, a useful short book. On the Church see now M. L. W. Laistner, *Christianity and Pagan Culture in the Later Roman Empire*, New York 1951; the earlier part of T. M. Parker, *Christianity and the State in the Light of History*, London 1955; W. Ullmann, *The Growth of Papal Government in the Middle Ages*, London 1955; and R. Folz, *L'Idée d'Empire en Occident du Ve au XIVe Siècle*, Paris 1953. E. Levy, *West Roman Vulgar Law*, Philadelphia 1951, opens a new field of study. In the social and economic fields see R. Latouche, *Les Origines de l'économie occidentale*, Paris 1957; A. R. Lewis, *Naval Power and Trade in the Mediterranean*, A.D. 500–1100, Princeton 1951; C. Verlinden, *L'Esclavage dans L' Europe Médiévale*, vol. I (Spain-France), Bruges 1955; and F. L. Ganshof, *Feudalism* (trs. P. Grierson), London 1952. E. A. Thompson, *A History of Attila and the Huns*, Oxford 1948, is very able. On Africa there is now W.H.C. Frend, *The Donatist Church*, Oxford 1952; C. Courtois, *Les Vandales et l'Afrique*, Paris 1955; and the same author's *Victor de Vita et son œuvre*, Algiers 1954. Nora K. Chadwick's *Poetry and Letters in Early Christian Gaul*, London 1955, is a good introduction; C. Verlinden, *Les Origines de la Frontière Linguistique en Belgique et la Colonisation Franque*, Brussels 1955, a neat survey of a big problem; G. W. Greenaway, *Saint Boniface*, London 1955, a scholarly essay. P. Goubert, *Byzance avant d'Islam*, vol. 2, Paris 1956, deals with Frankish-Byzantine relations. The earlier part of J. M. Wallace-Hadrill and J. McManners (edd.), *France, Government and Society*, London 1957, may be found of interest, also O. Chadwick, *John Cassian*, Cambridge 1950.

The following articles are recommended:

On the military implications of the barbarian assaults see now A. H. M. Jones, "The Decline and Fall of the Roman Empire", *History*, XL, 1955; E. A. Thompson, "The Passio S. Sabae and Early Visigothic Society", *Historia*, vol. 4, 1955; A. Momigliano, "Cassiodorus and Italian Culture of His Time", *British Academy Proceedings*, 1955; W. H C. Frend, "North Africa and Europe in the Early Middle Ages", Trans. R. Hist. Soc., 1955.

I continue to exclude books written in languages other than English and French, though in German particularly there is much important work on the period.

INDEX

A

Adalard, 123
Admonitio Generalis, 103–104
Adrianople, 21
Adso of Montiérender, 145
Aethelberht of Kent, 54, 103
Aetius, 26, 27, 28
Africa, 16, 23, 24, 26, 37, 38, 40, 41, 42
African Church, 39
Agilulf, 53, 54, 55
Agobard of Lyon, 94, 122
Aignan, Saint, of Orleans, 28
Aistulf, 58, 64, 97
Aix-la-Chapelle (Aachen), 48, 109, 116, 119, 121, 127
Alamans (Alamanni), 21, 68, 73, 86, 90
Alaric, 22, 23, 38
——II, 74
Alboin, 45, 46, 47, 62
Alcuin, 93, 105, 107, 108, 113, 114, 116, 132
aldio, 61
Amalaric, Visigothic King, 77
Amalfi, 137
Amand, Saint, 85
Ambrose, Saint, 16, 17, 18, 35
Ammianus Marcellinus, 67
Amorbach, 106
Amöneburg, monastery of, 87
Anastasius I, Emperor, 74
Andenne, community of, 85
Anglo-Saxons, 53; 94, 101, 128, 134
Annals, Frankish, 92, 95, 101, 130, 131, 134, 136
Annapes, 117
Anskar, Saint, of Corbie, 134
Antioch, 14
antrustion, 111
Aquileia, 29, 54
Aquitaine (Aquitania), 25, 26, 74, 82, 83, 89, 90, 98, 99, 100, 119, 121, 123, 125

Arabs (Saracens, Islam), 42, 81, 89, 90, 98, 99, 114, 116, 118, 119, 122, 137–8
Ardennes, 84, 101
Ardo, 122
Arianism, 13, 22, 30, 54, 55, 56, 69, 73
Arians, 16, 25, 28, 29, 33, 36, 37, 38, 39, 41, 45, 72, 77, 78
Arius, 23
Arnulf, Saint, of Metz, 43, 80, 84
——Archbishop of Reims, 144
Aspar, 40
Athens, 17
Athaulf, 25
Attila, 28, 30, 31, 33, 70, 139
Augustine, Saint, of Hippo, 15, 16, 17, 18, 19, 30, 35, 39, 50, 52, 60, 101, 103, 104, 107, 130
Augustus, 9, 14, 16, 39
Augsburg, 88
Austrasia, 77–8, 83, 86, 90, 95, 96, 101; Austrasians, 80, 82, 85, 87
Authari, 54
Avars, 45, 82–3, 100, 105, 113, 114, 139

B

Bagaudae, 66
Bâle, 88
bannum, 111
Barbarian Law, 55, 56
Basil, Saint, Rule of, 64
Basina, Queen, 83–4
Basques (Gascons), 90, 99
Bavaria, Bavarians, 54, 78, 83, 86, 88, 90, 100, 101, 114, 123, 140, 142
Bede, 69, 107, 132, 141
Begga, Saint, 85
Belisarius, 41, 52
Belgica Secunda, 46, 67, 72

151

BRITANNIA

NEUSTRIA

AQUITANIA

VASCONIA

HISPANIA

Laon

Soissons

Verdun

BUR

PROV

"GEOGRAPHIA" LTD.

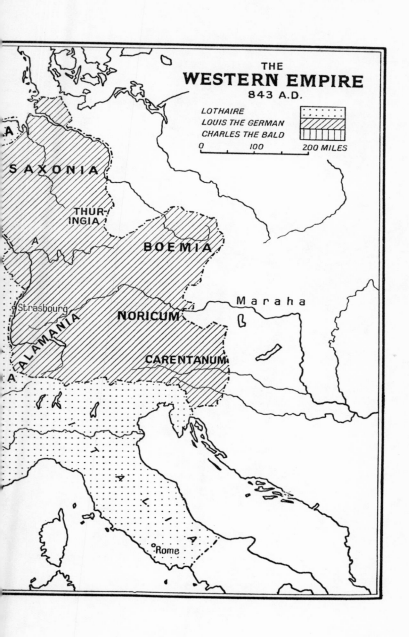

THE
WESTERN EMPIRE
843 A.D.

LOTHAIRE
LOUIS THE GERMAN
CHARLES THE BALD

0   100   200 MILES

A

SAXONIA

THUR-
INGIA

A

BOEMIA

Strasbourg

NORICUM

ALAMANIA

CARENTANUM

Maraha

A

Rome

Revised December, 1967

hARPER ⚜ ⊙ORChBOOKS

HUMANITIES AND SOCIAL SCIENCES

American Studies: General

LOUIS D. BRANDEIS: Other People's Money, and How the Bankers Use It. ‡ Ed. with an Intro. by Richard M. Abrams   TB/3081
THOMAS C. COCHRAN: The Inner Revolution. Essays on the Social Sciences in History   TB/1140
HENRY STEELE COMMAGER, Ed.: The Struggle for Racial Equality   TB/1300
EDWARD S. CORWIN: American Constitutional History. Essays edited by Alpheus T. Mason and Gerald Garvey △   TB/1136
CARL N. DEGLER, Ed.: Pivotal Interpretations of American History   Vol. I TB/1240; Vol. II TB/1241
A. HUNTER DUPREE: Science in the Federal Government: A History of Policies and Activities to 1940   TB/573
A. S. EISENSTADT, Ed.: The Craft of American History: Recent Essays in American Historical Writing
                        Vol. I TB/1255; Vol. II TB/1256
CHARLOTTE P. GILMAN: Women and Economics: A Study of the Economic Relation between Men and Women as a Factor in Social Evolution. ‡ Ed. with an Introduction by Carl N. Degler   TB/3073
OSCAR HANDLIN, Ed.: This Was America: As Recorded by European Travelers in the Eighteenth, Nineteenth and Twentieth Centuries. Illus.   TB/1119
MARCUS LEE HANSEN: The Atlantic Migration: 1607-1860. Edited by Arthur M. Schlesinger   TB/1052
MARCUS LEE HANSEN: The Immigrant in American History.   TB/1120
JOHN HIGHAM, Ed.: The Reconstruction of American History △   TB/1068
ROBERT H. JACKSON: The Supreme Court in the American System of Government   TB/1106
JOHN F. KENNEDY: A Nation of Immigrants. △ Illus.
                                             TB/1118
LEONARD W. LEVY, Ed.: American Constitutional Law: Historical Essays   TB/1285
LEONARD W. LEVY, Ed.: Judicial Review and the Supreme Court   TB/1296
LEONARD W. LEVY: The Law of the Commonwealth and Chief Justice Shaw   TB/1309
HENRY F. MAY: Protestant Churches and Industrial America. New Intro. by the Author   TB/1334
RALPH BARTON PERRY: Puritanism and Democracy
                                             TB/1138
ARNOLD ROSE: The Negro in America   TB/3048
MAURICE R. STEIN: The Eclipse of Community. An Interpretation of American Studies   TB/1128
W. LLOYD WARNER and Associates: Democracy in Jonesville: A Study in Quality and Inequality ¶   TB/1129
W. LLOYD WARNER: Social Class in America: The Evaluation of Status   TB/1013

American Studies: Colonial

BERNARD BAILYN, Ed.: Apologia of Robert Keayne: Self-Portrait of a Puritan Merchant   TB/1201
BERNARD BAILYN: The New England Merchants in the Seventeenth Century   TB/1149
JOSEPH CHARLES: The Origins of the American Party System   TB/1049
HENRY STEELE COMMAGER & ELMO GIORDANETTI, Eds.: Was America a Mistake? An Eighteenth Century Controversy   TB/1329
CHARLES GIBSON: Spain in America †   TB/3077
LAWRENCE HENRY GIPSON: The Coming of the Revolution: 1763-1775. † Illus.   TB/3007
LEONARD W. LEVY: Freedom of Speech and Press in Early American History: Legacy of Suppression TB/1109
PERRY MILLER: Errand Into the Wilderness   TB/1139
PERRY MILLER & T. H. JOHNSON, Eds.: The Puritans: A Sourcebook of Their Writings
                        Vol. I TB/1093; Vol. II TB/1094
EDMUND S. MORGAN, Ed.: The Diary of Michael Wigglesworth, 1653-1657: The Conscience of a Puritan
                                             TB/1228
EDMUND S. MORGAN: The Puritan Family: Religion and Domestic Relations in Seventeenth-Century New England   TB/1227
RICHARD B. MORRIS: Government and Labor in Early America   TB/1244
KENNETH B. MURDOCK: Literature and Theology in Colonial New England   TB/99
WALLACE NOTESTEIN: The English People on the Eve of Colonization: 1603-1630. † Illus.   TB/3006
JOHN P. ROCHE: Origins of American Political Thought: Selected Readings   TB/1301
JOHN SMITH: Captain John Smith's America: Selections from His Writings. Ed. with Intro. by John Lankford
                                             TB/3078
LOUIS B. WRIGHT: The Cultural Life of the American Colonies: 1607-1763. † Illus.   TB/3005

American Studies: From the Revolution to 1860

JOHN R. ALDEN: The American Revolution: 1775-1783. † Illus.   TB/3011
MAX BELOFF, Ed.: The Debate on the American Revolution, 1761-1783: A Sourcebook △   TB/1225
RAY A. BILLINGTON: The Far Western Frontier: 1830-1860. † Illus.   TB/3012
EDMUND BURKE: On the American Revolution: Selected Speeches and Letters. ‡ Edited by Elliott Robert Barkan   TB/3068
WHITNEY R. CROSS: The Burned-Over District: The Social and Intellectual History of Enthusiastic Religion in Western New York, 1800-1850 △   TB/1242
GEORGE DANGERFIELD: The Awakening of American Nationalism; 1815-1828. † Illus.   TB/3061

† The New American Nation Series, edited by Henry Steele Commager and Richard B. Morris.
‡ American Perspectives series, edited by Bernard Wishy and William E. Leuchtenburg.
* The Rise of Modern Europe series, edited by William L. Langer.
** History of Europe series, edited by J. H. Plumb.
¶ Researches in the Social, Cultural and Behavioral Sciences, edited by Benjamin Nelson.
§ The Library of Religion and Culture, edited by Benjamin Nelson.
Ƶ Harper Modern Science Series, edited by James R. Newman.
° Not for sale in Canada.
△ Not for sale in the U. K.

CLEMENT EATON: The Freedom-of-Thought Struggle in the Old South. *Revised and Enlarged. Illus.* TB/1150

CLEMENT EATON: The Growth of Southern Civilization: 1790-1860. † *Illus.* TB/3040

LOUIS FILLER: The Crusade Against Slavery: 1830-1860. † *Illus.* TB/3029

DIXON RYAN FOX: The Decline of Aristocracy in the Politics of New York: 1801-1840. ‡ *Edited by Robert V. Remini* TB/3064

WILLIAM W. FREEHLING, Ed.: The Nullification Era: *A Documentary Record* ‡ TB/3079

FELIX GILBERT: The Beginnings of American Foreign Policy: *To the Farewell Address* TB/1200

FRANCIS GRIERSON: The Valley of Shadows: *The Coming of the Civil War in Lincoln's Midwest: A Contemporary Account* TB/1246

FRANCIS J. GRUND: Aristocracy in America: *Social Class in the Formative Years of the New Nation* TB/1001

ALEXANDER HAMILTON: The Reports of Alexander Hamilton. ‡ *Edited by Jacob E. Cooke* TB/3060

THOMAS JEFFERSON: Notes on the State of Virginia. ‡ *Edited by Thomas P. Abernethy* TB/3052

JAMES MADISON: The Forging of American Federalism: *Selected Writings of James Madison. Edited by Saul K. Padover* TB/1226

BERNARD MAYO: Myths and Men: *Patrick Henry, George Washington, Thomas Jefferson* TB/1108

JOHN C. MILLER: Alexander Hamilton and the Growth of the New Nation TB/3057

RICHARD B. MORRIS, Ed.: The Era of the American Revolution TB/1180

R. B. NYE: The Cultural Life of the New Nation: 1776-1801. † *Illus.* TB/3026

JAMES PARTON: The Presidency of Andrew Jackson. *From Vol. III of the Life of Andrew Jackson.* ‡ *Ed. with an Intro. by Robert V. Remini* TB/3080

FRANCIS S. PHILBRICK: The Rise of the West, 1754-1830. † *Illus.* TB/3067

TIMOTHY L. SMITH: Revivalism and Social Reform: *American Protestantism on the Eve of the Civil War* TB/1229

ALBION W. TOURGÉE: A Fool's Errand. ‡ *Ed. by George Fredrickson* TB/3074

A. F. TYLER: Freedom's Ferment: *Phases of American Social History from the Revolution to the Outbreak of the Civil War. 31 illus.* TB/1074

GLYNDON G. VAN DEUSEN: The Jacksonian Era: 1828-1848. † *Illus.* TB/3028

LOUIS B. WRIGHT: Culture on the Moving Frontier TB/1053

American Studies: The Civil War to 1900

W. R. BROCK: An American Crisis: Congress and Reconstruction, 1865-67 ○ △ TB/1283

THOMAS C. COCHRAN & WILLIAM MILLER: The Age of Enterprise: *A Social History of Industrial America* TB/1054

W. A. DUNNING: Essays on the Civil War and Reconstruction. *Introduction by David Donald* TB/1181

W. A. DUNNING: Reconstruction, Political and Economic: 1865-1877 TB/1073

HAROLD U. FAULKNER: Politics, Reform and Expansion: 1890-1900. † *Illus.* TB/3020

HELEN HUNT JACKSON: A Century of Dishonor: *The Early Crusade for Indian Reform.* ‡ *Edited by Andrew F. Rolle* TB/3063

ALBERT D. KIRWAN: Revolt of the Rednecks: *Mississippi Politics, 1876-1925* TB/1199

ROBERT GREEN MC CLOSKEY: American Conservatism in the Age of Enterprise: 1865-1910 TB/1137

ARTHUR MANN: Yankee Reformers in the Urban Age: *Social Reform in Boston, 1880-1900* TB/1247

WHITELAW REID: After the War: *A Tour of the Southern States, 1865-1866.* ‡ *Edited by C. Vann Woodward* TB/3066

CHARLES H. SHINN: Mining Camps: *A Study in American Frontier Government.* ‡ *Edited by Rodman W. Paul* TB/3062

VERNON LANE WHARTON: The Negro in Mississippi: 1865-1890 TB/1178

American Studies: 1900 to the Present

RAY STANNARD BAKER: Following the Color Line: *American Negro Citizenship in Progressive Era.* ‡ *Illus. Edited by Dewey W. Grantham, Jr.* TB/3053

RANDOLPH S. BOURNE: War and the Intellectuals: *Collected Essays, 1915-1919.* ‡ *Edited by Carl Resek* TB/3043

A. RUSSELL BUCHANAN: The United States and World War II. † *Illus.* Vol. I TB/3044; Vol. II TB/3045

ABRAHAM CAHAN: The Rise of David Levinsky: *a documentary novel of social mobility in early twentieth century America. Intro. by John Higham* TB/1028

THOMAS C. COCHRAN: The American Business System: *A Historical Perspective, 1900-1955* TB/1080

FOSTER RHEA DULLES: America's Rise to World Power: 1898-1954. † *Illus.* TB/3021

JOHN D. HICKS: Republican Ascendancy: 1921-1933. † *Illus.* TB/3041

SIDNEY HOOK: Reason, Social Myths, and Democracy TB/1237

ROBERT HUNTER: Poverty: *Social Conscience in the Progressive Era.* ‡ *Edited by Peter d'A. Jones* TB/3065

WILLIAM L. LANGER & S. EVERETT GLEASON: The Challenge to Isolation: *The World Crisis of 1937-1940 and American Foreign Policy* Vol. I TB/3054; Vol. II TB/3055

WILLIAM E. LEUCHTENBURG: Franklin D. Roosevelt and the New Deal: 1932-1940. † *Illus.* TB/3025

ARTHUR S. LINK: Woodrow Wilson and the Progressive Era: 1910-1917. † *Illus.* TB/3023

GEORGE E. MOWRY: The Era of Theodore Roosevelt and the Birth of Modern America: 1900-1912. † *Illus.* TB/3022

RUSSEL B. NYE: Midwestern Progressive Politics: *A Historical Study of Its Origins and Development, 1870-1958* TB/1202

WILLIAM PRESTON, JR.: Aliens and Dissenters: *Federal Suppression of Radicals, 1903-1933* TB/1287

WALTER RAUSCHENBUSCH: Christianity and the Social Crisis. ‡ *Edited by Robert D. Cross* TB/3059

JACOB RIIS: The Making of an American. ‡ *Edited by Roy Lubove* TB/3070

PHILIP SELZNICK: TVA and the Grass Roots: *A Study in the Sociology of Formal Organization* TB/1230

IDA M. TARBELL: The History of the Standard Oil Company: *Briefer Version.* ‡ *Edited by David M. Chalmers* TB/3071

GEORGE B. TINDALL, Ed.: A Populist Reader ‡ TB/3069

TWELVE SOUTHERNERS: I'll Take My Stand: *The South and the Agrarian Tradition. Intro. by Louis D. Rubin, Jr., Biographical Essays by Virginia Rock* TB/1072

Anthropology

JACQUES BARZUN: Race: *A Study in Superstition. Revised Edition* TB/1172

JOSEPH B. CASAGRANDE, Ed.: In the Company of Man: *Twenty Portraits of Anthropological Informants. Illus.* TB/3047

W. E. LE GROS CLARK: The Antecedents of Man: *Intro. to Evolution of the Primates.* ○ △ *Illus.* TB/559

CORA DU BOIS: The People of Alor. *New Preface by the author. Illus.* Vol. I TB/1042; Vol. II TB/1043

RAYMOND FIRTH, Ed.: Man and Culture: *An Evaluation of the Work of Bronislaw Malinowski* ¶ ○ △ TB/1133

DAVID LANDY: Tropical Childhood: *Cultural Transmission and Learning in a Puerto Rican Village* ¶ TB/1235

L. S. B. LEAKEY: Adam's Ancestors: *The Evolution of Man and His Culture.* △ *Illus.* TB/1019

EDWARD BURNETT TYLOR: Religion in Primitive Culture. Part II of "Primitive Culture." § *Intro. by Paul Radin* TB/34

W. LLOYD WARNER: A Black Civilization: *A Study of an Australian Tribe.* ¶ *Illus.* TB/3056

Art and Art History

WALTER LOWRIE: Art in the Early Church. *Revised Edition. 452 illus.* TB/124

EMILE MÂLE: The Gothic Image: *Religious Art in France of the Thirteenth Century.* § △ *190 illus.* TB/44

MILLARD MEISS: Painting in Florence and Siena after the Black Death: *The Arts, Religion and Society in the Mid-Fourteenth Century. 169 illus.* TB/1148

ERICH NEUMANN: The Archetypal World of Henry Moore. △ *107 illus.* TB/2020

DORA & ERWIN PANOFSKY : Pandora's Box: *The Changing Aspects of a Mythical Symbol. Revised Edition. Illus.* TB/2021

ERWIN PANOFSKY: Studies in Iconology: *Humanistic Themes in the Art of the Renaissance.* △ *180 illustrations* TB/1077

ALEXANDRE PIANKOFF: The Shrines of Tut-Ankh-Amon. *Edited by N. Rambova. 117 illus.* TB/2011

JEAN SEZNEC: The Survival of the Pagan Gods: *The Mythological Tradition and Its Place in Renaissance Humanism and Art. 108 illustrations* TB/2004

OTTO VON SIMSON: The Gothic Cathedral: *Origins of Gothic Architecture and the Medieval Concept of Order.* △ *58 illus.* TB/2018

HEINRICH ZIMMER: Myth and Symbols in Indian Art and Civilization. *70 illustrations* TB/2005

Business, Economics & Economic History

REINHARD BENDIX: Work and Authority in Industry: *Ideologies of Management in the Course of Industrialization* TB/3035

GILBERT BURCK & EDITORS OF FORTUNE: The Computer Age: *And Its Potential for Management* TB/1179

THOMAS C. COCHRAN: The American Business System: *A Historical Perspective, 1900-1955* TB/1080

THOMAS C. COCHRAN: The Inner Revolution: *Essays on the Social Sciences in History* △ TB/1140

THOMAS C. COCHRAN & WILLIAM MILLER: The Age of Enterprise: *A Social History of Industrial America* TB/1054

ROBERT DAHL & CHARLES E. LINDBLOM: Politics, Economics, and Welfare: *Planning and Politico-Economic Systems Resolved into Basic Social Processes* TB/3037

PETER F. DRUCKER: The New Society: *The Anatomy of Industrial Order* △ TB/1082

EDITORS OF FORTUNE: America in the Sixties: *The Economy and the Society* TB/1015

ROBERT L. HEILBRONER: The Great Ascent: *The Struggle for Economic Development in Our Time* TB/3030

ROBERT L. HEILBRONER: The Limits of American Capitalism TB/1305

FRANK H. KNIGHT: The Economic Organization TB/1214

FRANK H. KNIGHT: Risk, Uncertainty and Profit TB/1215

ABBA P. LERNER: Everybody's Business: *Current Assumptions in Economics and Public Policy* TB/3051

ROBERT GREEN MC CLOSKEY: American Conservatism in the Age of Enterprise, 1865-1910 △ TB/1137

PAUL MANTOUX: The Industrial Revolution in the Eighteenth Century: *The Beginnings of the Modern Factory System in England* ◦ △ TB/1079

WILLIAM MILLER, Ed.: Men in Business: *Essays on the Historical Role of the Entrepreneur* TB/1081

RICHARD B. MORRIS: Government and Labor in Early America △ TB/1244

HERBERT SIMON: The Shape of Automation: *For Men and Management* TB/1245

PERRIN STRYKER: The Character of the Executive: *Eleven Studies in Managerial Qualities* TB/1041

Education

JACQUES BARZUN: The House of Intellect △ TB/1051

RICHARD M. JONES, Ed.: Contemporary Educational Psychology: *Selected Readings* TB/1292

CLARK KERR: The Uses of the University TB/1264

JOHN U. NEF: Cultural Foundations of Industrial Civilization △ TB/1024

Historiography & Philosophy of History

JACOB BURCKHARDT: On History and Historians. △ *Introduction by H. R. Trevor-Roper* TB/1216

WILHELM DILTHEY: Pattern and Meaning in History: *Thoughts on History and Society.* ◦ △ *Edited with an Introduction by H. P. Rickman* TB/1075

J. H. HEXTER: Reappraisals in History: *New Views on History & Society in Early Modern Europe* △ TB/1100

H. STUART HUGHES: History as Art and as Science: *Twin Vistas on the Past* TB/1207

RAYMOND KLIBANSKY & H. J. PATON, Eds.: Philosophy and History: *The Ernst Cassirer Festschrift. Illus.* TB/1115

ARNALDO MOMIGLIANO: Studies in Historiography ◦ △ TB/1283

GEORGE H. NADEL, Ed.: Studies in the Philosophy of History: *Selected Essays from History and Theory* TB/1208

JOSE ORTEGA Y GASSET: The Modern Theme. *Introduction by Jose Ferrater Mora* TB/1038

KARL R. POPPER: The Open Society and Its Enemies △
Vol. I: The Spell of Plato TB/1101
Vol. II: The High Tide of Prophecy: Hegel, Marx and the Aftermath TB/1102

KARL R. POPPER: The Poverty of Historicism ◦ △ TB/1126

G. J. RENIER: History: Its Purpose and Method △ TB/1209

W. H. WALSH: Philosophy of History: *An Introduction* △ TB/1020

History: General

WOLFGANG FRANKE: China and the West. *Trans by R. A. Wilson* TB/1326

L. CARRINGTON GOODRICH: A Short History of the Chinese People. △ *Illus.* TB/3015

DAN N. JACOBS & HANS H. BAERWALD: Chinese Communism: *Selected Documents* TB/3031

BERNARD LEWIS: The Arabs in History △ TB/1029

BERNARD LEWIS: The Middle East and the West ◦ △ TB/1274

History: Ancient

A. ANDREWES: The Greek Tyrants △ TB/1103

ADOLF ERMAN, Ed. The Ancient Egyptians: *A Sourcebook of Their Writings. New material and Introduction by William Kelly Simpson* TB/1233

MICHAEL GRANT: Ancient History ◦ △ TB/1190

SAMUEL NOAH KRAMER: Sumerian Mythology TB/1055

NAPHTALI LEWIS & MEYER REINHOLD, Eds.: Roman Civilization. *Sourcebook I: The Republic* TB/1231

NAPHTALI LEWIS & MEYER REINHOLD, Eds.: Roman Civilization. *Sourcebook II: The Empire* TB/1232

History: Medieval

P. BOISSONNADE: Life and Work in Medieval Europe: *The Evolution of the Medieval Economy, the 5th to the 15th Century.* ◦ △ *Preface by Lynn White, Jr.* TB/1141

HELEN CAM: England before Elizabeth △ TB/1026

NORMAN COHN: The Pursuit of the Millennium: *Revolutionary Messianism in Medieval and Reformation Europe* △ TB/1037

3

C. G. JUNG & C. KERÉNYI: Essays on a Science of Mythology: *The Myths of the Divine Child and the Divine Maiden* TB/2014

DORA & ERWIN PANOFSKY : Pandora's Box: *The Changing Aspects of a Mythical Symbol.* △ *Revised edition. Illus.* TB/2021

ERWIN PANOFSKY: Studies in Iconology: *Humanistic Themes in the Art of the Renaissance.* △ *180 illustrations* TB/1077

JEAN SEZNEC: The Survival of the Pagan Gods: *The Mythological Tradition and its Place in Renaissance Humanism and Art.* △ *108 illustrations* TB/2004

HELLMUT WILHELM: Change: *Eight Lectures on the I Ching* △ TB/2019

HEINRICH ZIMMER: Myths and Symbols in Indian Art and Civilization. △ *70 illustrations* TB/2005

Philosophy

G. E. M. ANSCOMBE: An Introduction to Wittgenstein's Tractatus. ○ △ *Second Edition, Revised* TB/1210

HENRI BERGSON: Time and Free Will: *An Essay on the Immediate Data of Consciousness* ○ △ TB/1021

H. J. BLACKHAM: Six Existentialist Thinkers: *Kierkegaard, Nietzsche, Jaspers, Marcel, Heidegger, Sartre* ○ △ TB/1002

CRANE BRINTON: Nietzsche. *New Preface, Bibliography and Epilogue by the Author* TB/1197

MARTIN BUBER: The Knowledge of Man. △ *Ed. with an Intro. by Maurice Friedman. Trans. by Maurice Friedman and Ronald Gregor Smith* TB/135

ERNST CASSIRER: The Individual and the Cosmos in Renaissance Philosophy. △ *Translated with an Introduction by Mario Domandi* TB/1097

ERNST CASSIRER: Rousseau, Kant and Goethe. *Introduction by Peter Gay* TB/1092

FREDERICK COPLESTON: Medieval Philosophy ○ △ TB/376

F. M. CORNFORD: Principium Sapientiae: *A Study of the Origins of Greek Philosophical Thought. Edited by W. K. C. Guthrie* TB/1213

F. M. CORNFORD: From Religion to Philosophy: *A Study in the Origins of Western Speculation* § TB/20

WILFRID DESAN: The Tragic Finale: *An Essay on the Philosophy of Jean-Paul Sartre* TB/1030

A. P. D'ENTRÈVES: Natural Law: *An Historical Survey* △ TB/1223

MARVIN FARBER: The Aims of Phenomenology: *The Motives, Methods, and Impact of Husserl's Thought* TB/1291

MARVIN FARBER: Phenomenology and Existence: *Towards a Philosophy within Nature* TB/1295

HERBERT FINGARETTE: The Self in Transformation: *Psychoanalysis, Philosophy and the Life of the Spirit* ¶ TB/1177

PAUL FRIEDLÄNDER: Plato: *An Introduction* △ TB/2017

J. GLENN GRAY: The Warriors: *Reflections on Men in Battle. Intro. by Hannah Arendt* TB/1294

WILLIAM CHASE GREENE: Moira: *Fate, Good, and Evil in Greek Thought* TB/1104

W. K. C. GUTHRIE: The Greek Philosophers: *From Thales to Aristotle* ○ △ TB/1008

G. W. F. HEGEL: The Phenomenology of Mind ○ △ TB/1303

F. H. HEINEMANN: Existentialism and the Modern Predicament △ TB/28

ISAAC HUSIK: A History of Medieval Jewish Philosophy JP/3

EDMUND HUSSERL: Phenomenology and the Crisis of Philosophy. *Translated with an Introduction by Quentin Lauer* TB/1170

IMMANUEL KANT: The Doctrine of Virtue, *being Part II of the Metaphysic of Morals. Trans. with Notes & Intro. by Mary J. Gregor. Foreword by H. J. Paton* TB/110

IMMANUEL KANT: Groundwork of the Metaphysic of Morals. *Trans. & analyzed by H. J. Paton* TB/1159

IMMANUEL KANT: Lectures on Ethics. § △ *Introduction by Lewis W. Beck* TB/105

IMMANUEL KANT: Religion Within the Limits of Reason Alone. § *Intro. by T. M. Greene & J. Silber* TB/67

QUENTIN LAUER: Phenomenology: *Its Genesis and Prospect* TB/1169

MAURICE MANDELBAUM: The Problem of Historical Knowledge: *An Answer to Relativism. New Preface by the Author* TB/1338

GABRIEL MARCEL: Being and Having: *An Existential Diary.* △ *Intro. by James Collins* TB/310

GEORGE A. MORGAN: What Nietzsche Means TB/1198

H. J. PATON: The Categorical Imperative: *A Study in Kant's Moral Philosophy* △ TB/1325

PHILO, SAADYA GAON, & JEHUDA HALEVI: Three Jewish Philosophers. *Ed. by Hans Lewy, Alexander Altmann, &Isaak Heinemann* TB/813

MICHAEL POLANYI: Personal Knowledge: *Towards a Post-Critical Philosophy* △ TB/1158

WILLARD VAN ORMAN QUINE: Elementary Logic: *Revised Edition* TB/577

WILLARD VAN ORMAN QUINE: From a Logical Point of View: *Logico-Philosophical Essays* TB/566

BERTRAND RUSSELL et al.: The Philosophy of Bertrand Russell. *Edited by Paul Arthur Schilpp*
Vol. I TB/1095; Vol. II TB/1096

L. S. STEBBING: A Modern Introduction to Logic △ TB/538

ALFRED NORTH WHITEHEAD: Process and Reality: *An Essay in Cosmology* △ TB/1033

PHILIP P. WIENER: Evolution and the Founders of Pragmatism. *Foreword by John Dewey* TB/1212

WILHELM WINDELBAND: A History of Philosophy
Vol. I: *Greek, Roman, Medieval* TB/38
Vol. II: *Renaissance, Enlightenment, Modern* TB/39

LUDWIG WITTGENSTEIN: The Blue and Brown Books ○ TB/1211

Political Science & Government

JEREMY BENTHAM: The Handbook of Political Fallacies: *Introduction by Crane Brinton* TB/1069

C. E. BLACK: The Dynamics of Modernization: *A Study in Comparative History* TB/1321

KENNETH E. BOULDING: Conflict and Defense: *A General Theory* TB/3024

CRANE BRINTON: English Political Thought in the Nineteenth Century TB/1071

ROBERT CONQUEST: Power and Policy in the USSR: *The Study of Soviet Dynastics* △ TB/1307

EDWARD S. CORWIN: American Constitutional History: *Essays edited by Alpheus T. Mason and Gerald Garvey* TB/1136

ROBERT DAHL & CHARLES E. LINDBLOM: Politics, Economics, and Welfare: *Planning and Politico-Economic Systems Resolved into Basic Social Processes* TB/3037

JOHN NEVILLE FIGGIS: The Divine Right of Kings. *Introduction by G. R. Elton* TB/1191

JOHN NEVILLE FIGGIS: Political Thought from Gerson to Grotius: 1414-1625: *Seven Studies. Introduction by Garrett Mattingly* TB/1032

F. L. GANSHOF: Feudalism △ TB/1058

G. P. GOOCH: English Democratic Ideas in the Seventeenth Century TB/1006

J. H. HEXTER: More's Utopia: *The Biography of an Idea. New Epilogue by the Author* TB/1195

SIDNEY HOOK: Reason, Social Myths and Democracy △ TB/1237

ROBERT H. JACKSON: The Supreme Court in the American System of Government △ TB/1106

DAN N. JACOBS, Ed.: The New Communist Manifesto *and Related Documents. Third Edition, Revised* TB/1078

DAN N. JACOBS & HANS BAERWALD, Eds.: Chinese Communism: *Selected Documents* TB/3031

7

Psychology

Sociology

PHILIP SELZNICK: TVA and the Grass Roots: *A Study in the Sociology of Formal Organization*   TB/1230

GEORG SIMMEL et al.: Essays on Sociology, Philosophy, and Aesthetics. ¶ *Edited by Kurt H. Wolff*   TB/1234

HERBERT SIMON: The Shape of Automation: *For Men and Management* △   TB/1245

PITIRIM A. SOROKIN: Contemporary Sociological Theories. *Through the First Quarter of the 20th Century* TB/3046

MAURICE R. STEIN: The Eclipse of Community: *An Interpretation of American Studies*   TB/1128

WILLIAM I. THOMAS: The Unadjusted Girl: *With Cases and Standpoint for Behavior Analysis*. ¶ *New Intro. by Michael Parenti*   TB/1319

EDWARD A. TIRYAKIAN, Ed.: Sociological Theory, Values and Sociocultural Change: *Essays in Honor of Pitirim A. Sorokin* ¶ △ ○   TB/1316

FERDINAND TÖNNIES: Community and Society: *Gemeinschaft und Gesellschaft. Translated and edited by Charles P. Loomis*   TB/1116

W. LLOYD WARNER & Associates: Democracy in Jonesville: *A Study in Quality and Inequality*   TB/1129

W. LLOYD WARNER: Social Class in America: *The Evaluation of Status* △   TB/1013

RELIGION

Ancient & Classical

J. H. BREASTED: Development of Religion and Thought in Ancient Egypt. *Intro. by John A. Wilson*   TB/57

HENRI FRANKFORT: Ancient Egyptian Religion: *An Interpretation*   TB/77

G. RACHEL LEVY: Religious Conceptions of the Stone Age *and their Influence upon European Thought*. △ *Illus. Introduction by Henri Frankfort*   TB/106

MARTIN P. NILSSON: Greek Folk Religion. *Foreword by Arthur Darby Nock*   TB/78

ALEXANDRE PIANKOFF: The Shrines of Tut-Ankh-Amon. ^ *Edited by N. Rambova. 117 illus.*   TB/2011

ERWIN ROHDE: Psyche: *The Cult of Souls and Belief in Immortality Among the Greeks*. △ *Intro. by W. K. C. Guthrie*   Vol. I TB/140; Vol. II TB/141

H. J. ROSE: Religion in Greece and Rome △   TB/55

Biblical Thought & Literature

W. F. ALBRIGHT: The Biblical Period from Abraham to Ezra   TB/102

C. K. BARRETT, Ed.: The New Testament Background: *Selected Documents* △   TB/86

C. H. DODD: The Authority of the Bible △   TB/43

M. S. ENSLIN: Christian Beginnings △   TB/5

M. S. ENSLIN: The Literature of the Christian Movement △   TB/6

JOHN GRAY: Archaeology and the Old Testament World. △ *Illus.*   TB/127

JAMES MUILENBURG: The Way of Israel: *Biblical Faith and Ethics* △   TB/133

H. H. ROWLEY: The Growth of the Old Testament △   TB/107

GEORGE ADAM SMITH: The Historical Geography of the Holy Land. ○ △ *Revised and reset*   TB/138

D. WINTON THOMAS, Ed.: Documents from Old Testament Times △   TB/85

WALTHER ZIMMERLI: The Law and the Prophets: *A Study of the Meaning of the Old Testament* △   TB/144

The Judaic Tradition

LEO BAECK: Judaism and Christianity. *Trans. with Intro. by Walter Kaufmann*   TB/823

SALO W. BARON: Modern Nationalism and Religion   TB/818

MARTIN BUBER: Eclipse of God: *Studies in the Relation Between Religion and Philosophy* △   TB/12

MARTIN BUBER: For the Sake of Heaven   TB/801

MARTIN BUBER: Hasidism and Modern Man. △ *Ed. and Trans. by Maurice Friedman*   TB/839

MARTIN BUBER: The Knowledge of Man. △ *Edited with an Introduction by Maurice Friedman. Translated by Maurice Friedman and Ronald Gregor Smith*   TB/135

MARTIN BUBER: Moses: *The Revelation and the Covenant* △   TB/837

MARTIN BUBER: The Origin and Meaning of Hasidism △   TB/835

MARTIN BUBER: Pointing the Way. △ *Introduction by Maurice S. Friedman*   TB/103

MARTIN BUBER: The Prophetic Faith   TB/73

MARTIN BUBER: Two Types of Faith: *the interpenetration of Judaism and Christianity* ○ △   TB/75

ERNST LUDWIG EHRLICH: A Concise History of Israel: *From the Earliest Times to the Destruction of the Temple in A.D. 70* ○ △   TB/128

MAURICE S. FRIEDMAN: Martin Buber: *The Life of Dialogue* △   TB/64

GENESIS: *The NJV Translation*   TB/836

SOLOMON GRAYZEL: A History of the Contemporary Jews   TB/816

WILL HERBERG: Judaism and Modern Man   TB/810

ARTHUR HERTZBERG: The Zionist Idea   TB/817

ABRAHAM J. HESCHEL: God in Search of Man: *A Philosophy of Judaism*   TB/807

ISAAC HUSIK: A History of Medieval Jewish Philosophy   TB/803

JACOB R. MARCUS: The Jew in the Medieval World TB/814

MAX L. MARGOLIS & ALEXANDER MARX: A History of the Jewish People   TB/806

T. J. MEEK: Hebrew Origins   TB/69

JAMES PARKES: The Conflict of the Church and the Synagogue: *The Jews and Early Christianity*   TB/821

PHILO, SAADYA GAON, & JEHUDA HALEVI: Three Jewish Philosophers. *Ed. by Hans Lewey, Alexander Altmann, & Isaak Heinemann*   TB/813

CECIL ROTH: A History of the Marranos   TB/812

CECIL ROTH: The Jews in the Renaissance. *Illus.* TB/834

HERMAN L. STRACK: Introduction to the Talmud and Midrash   TB/808

JOSHUA TRACHTENBERG: The Devil and the Jews: *The Medieval Conception of the Jew and its Relation to Modern Anti-Semitism*   TB/822

Christianity: General

ROLAND H. BAINTON: Christendom: *A Short History of Christianity and its Impact on Western Civilization*. △ *Illus.*   Vol. I TB/131; Vol. II TB/132

Christianity: Origins & Early Development

AUGUSTINE: An Augustine Synthesis. △ *Edited by Erich Przywara*   TB/335

W. D. DAVIES: Paul and Rabbinic Judaism: *Some Rabbinic Elements in Pauline Theology. New Intro. by the Author* △ ○   TB/146

ADOLF DEISSMANN: Paul: *A Study in Social and Religious History*   TB/15

EDWARD GIBBON: The Triumph of Christendom in the Roman Empire *(Chaps. XV-XX of "Decline and Fall," J. B. Bury edition)*. § △ *Illus.*   TB/46

EDGAR J. GOODSPEED: A Life of Jesus   TB/1

ROBERT M. GRANT: Gnosticism and Early Christianity. △ *Revised Edition*   TB/136

ADOLF HARNACK: The Mission and Expansion of Christianity in the First Three Centuries. *Introduction by Jaroslav Pelikan*   TB/92

R. K. HARRISON: The Dead Sea Scrolls : *An Introduction* ○ △   TB/84

EDWIN HATCH: The Influence of Greek Ideas on Christianity. § △ *Introduction and Bibliography by Frederick C. Grant*   TB/18

9

Oriental Religions: Far Eastern, Near Eastern

Philosophy of Religion

Religion, Culture & Society

NATURAL SCIENCES AND MATHEMATICS

Biological Sciences

Chemistry

Communication Theory

Geography

History of Science

A. G. VAN MELSEN: From Atomos to Atom: *A History of the Concept* Atom   TB/517
STEPHEN TOULMIN & JUNE GOODFIELD: The Architecture of Matter: *Physics, Chemistry & Physiology of Matter, Both Animate & Inanimate, As it Evolved Since the Beginning of Science* ° △   TB/584
STEPHEN TOULMIN & JUNE GOODFIELD: The Discovery of Time ° △   TB/585

Mathematics

E. W. BETH: The Foundations of Mathematics: *A Study in the Philosophy of Science* △   TB/581
S. KÖRNER: The Philosophy of Mathematics: *An Introduction* △   TB/547
GEORGE E. OWEN: Fundamentals of Scientific Mathematics   TB/569
WILLARD VAN ORMAN QUINE: Mathematical Logic TB/558
FREDERICK WAISMANN: Introduction to Mathematical Thinking. *Foreword by Karl Menger*   TB/511

Philosophy of Science

R. B. BRAITHWAITE: Scientific Explanation   TB/515

J. BRONOWSKI: Science and Human Values. △ *Revised and Enlarged Edition*   TB/505
ALBERT EINSTEIN et al.: Albert Einstein: Philosopher-Scientist. *Edited by Paul A. Schilpp*   Vol. I TB/502
                                             Vol. II TB/503
WERNER HEISENBERG: Physics and Philosophy: *The Revolution in Modern Science* △   TB/549
KARL R. POPPER: Logic of Scientific Discovery △   TB/576
STEPHEN TOULMIN: Foresight and Understanding: *An Enquiry into the Aims of Science.* △ *Foreword by Jacques Barzun*   TB/564
STEPHEN TOULMIN: The Philosophy of Science: *An Introduction* △   TB/513

Physics and Cosmology

JOHN E. ALLEN: Aerodynamics: *A Space Age Survey* △
                                                    TB/582
P. W. BRIDGMAN: Nature of Thermodynamics   TB/537
C. V. DURELL: Readable Relativity. △ *Foreword by Freeman J. Dyson*   TB/530
ARTHUR EDDINGTON: Space, Time and Gravitation: *An Outline of the General Relativity Theory*   TB/510
GEORGE GAMOW: Biography of Physics Σ △   TB/567
STEPHEN TOULMIN & JUNE GOODFIELD: The Fabric of the Heavens: *The Development of Astronomy and Dynamics.* △ *Illus.*   TB/579